The One Who Got Away

ESCAPE FROM THE KILL ROOM

By

Gilles Tetreault

The One Who Got Away © 2015 Gilles Tetreault

ISBN-13: 978-1539347736
ISBN-10: 1539347737

The information contained in this book is factual and based on true events. The author and publisher are in no way liable for misuse of the material.

Second Edition – 2016

Acknowledgements

I would like to thank the many people who have made this book possible.

First, to my parents and family that have always been there and that have supported me my entire life. To my son Benjamin, thank you for just being yourself. You make me smile every day and you make me proud to be a father. To Corrie Burge for the many hours of co-writing and editing that you put into the book. This book would not be the same without you. I wish you success on your new e-book "A Comedian's Adventures with MS (And Other Incurable Diseases)." To Bill Clark, the detectives involved, the Crown Prosecutors, and the victim services volunteers for working so hard on this case and helping me out when I needed it. Also I would like to thank Stolwijk Photography for the incredible author picture.

Thank you all!

Table of Contents

Chapter 1: Surreal

In the spring of 2011, my life was feeling more and more like an out of body experience. I never imagined I would ever be waiting to be interviewed for a primetime television audience, yet that's just where I found myself in May of that year. About to be interviewed by NBC, my mind drifted back to that night. I couldn't help but feel as if life and art were colliding again. It was surreal recollecting what happened to me, especially knowing that it would be shown on NBC and seen by countless people around the world. It felt like a dream, or a movie about someone *else's* struggle for their life.

As hard as it was to believe, my meeting with NBC was just the first in what would become a year filled with TV interviews. The following day, I was questioned in a local film studio for a joint collaboration between CBS and CBC. A couple of weeks later, I was on a plane to Los Angeles for three more days of interviews with NBC in Universal City. Two months later, I flew to New York City so I could be re-interviewed by CBS.

On the three-year anniversary of the attack, CBS came back to Edmonton to film some follow-up footage with me. As they filmed me playing with my son in a local park, I was filled with emotion knowing he wouldn't be here if I hadn't survived the attempt on my life. Then, it was just a few weeks later when the Biography Channel flew me out to L.A. so I could be interviewed. The final taped interview I would give about my testimony was for the Investigations Discovery Channel.

In the fall of 2011 the news specials began to play on TV and although filming the interviews had been strange, watching them back on TV felt much stranger. It felt like I was watching myself watch myself. The first taped interview ran in the fall of 2011 by *Dateline*. Shortly afterward, *The Fifth Estate* aired their program about the case called, "Murder, He Wrote". Yet another aired the early the next year when *48 Hours Mystery* aired their take on everything called, "A Screenplay for Murder". That summer the Investigations Discovery Channel featured me on their aptly named program, "Dates from Hell: Web of Seduction". In the fall the Biography Channel played an interview of me on, "I Survived".

When I was giving my interviews, I retold my story as if it had happened yesterday—in many ways it felt like it did. Flashbacks replayed images I cared not to remember, let alone relive for everyone on primetime television. Recreating it over and over again for each new audience, chills ran down my spine. With my thoughts returning to the attack repeatedly, I began seeing my attacker more often in the following weeks, months, and years. Even on the streets of New York City and Los Angeles, my mind couldn't help but lead me to believe I was seeing him everywhere. He was following me in cars, in line behind me at the grocery store, standing outside my house at night, and walking past studios and hotels in cities halfway across the country. It was like peering out the side of your shower curtain, expecting to see Norman Bates in your bathroom. I wish my story had been where it had all ended, but there was a different, more gruesome conclusion to it all. There is much more to this story; I was act one, part one, and "the *one* who got away" according to several media outlets.

Chapter 2: Trial Preparation

If I felt invaded by all the interviews; it was nothing compared to having the police come to take my personal computer. Even worse, they needed to look at communications I had on the dating website, Plenty of Fish. Weeks later, they still hadn't called me back about it. There is nowhere to hide when you are part of a homicide investigation. I was hoping they were done with it but hadn't gotten around to calling me to have me pick it up. Even though I had no idea what's really involved in an investigation like this, I knew that the Homicide Detectives in Edmonton were some of the busiest in the country and I didn't want to bother them with my trivial concerns about my second computer. After all, Edmonton, Alberta, aka "Deadmonton", has one of the highest murder rates in the country.

When Detective Kerr finally called to say I could go in and pick up my computer, he also informed me that I would have to meet with the Crown Prosecutors. He said a date was set for a meeting on in March 2009. Detective Kerr also asked me if I would be willing to give them a blood sample so they could use my DNA to match it to any blood they might find on the mask, or in the garage. Lastly, Detective Kerr also mentioned that I should park in the Edmonton Police Parking lot when I got there so that I didn't have to pay.

As I was driving to the police station, I realized that I had no idea where their private parking lot was. Not wanting to park in the incorrect place, I decided to pay for parking across the street. It was the same place I had parked the first time I met with the Edmonton Homicide Department. Putting my money in the meter, I remembered the day I gave my taped testimony to Detective Clark on November 3, 2008. It had been the day after I learned about John's murder. The interview had been intense and had lasted hours, but everyone had been incredibly kind to me. I grabbed the ticket, put it on my dashboard, locked my doors and crossed the street.

Slightly more comfortable this time, I called Detective Kerr to let him know I was in the waiting room, bypassing the front desk. I sat and waited in the exact same chairs I had while waiting for Detective Anstey to bring me to meet Detective Clark. It was only weeks ago but now it seemed like a lifetime away. After waiting for a few minutes, I saw Detective Kerr come through the doors. He thanked me for coming and said he would take me to meet the Crown Prosecutors. We walked to the John E. Brownlee Building, just across the street where we met Avril Ingles and Lawrence Van Dyke in Avril's sixth floor office. My first impressions were extremely positive, sensing that they were extraordinarily nice people. Avril shook my hand, saying she had watched my police video testimony and was enthralled with my story. She told me I was lucky to be alive, given what I went through. Both she and Lawrence set me at ease, helping me forget where I was and what I was there for, at least for a moment.

I was happy with everything the Prosecutors said, up until Avril told me she would have to release my name in the court documents in order to charge Twitchell for attempted murder. Worriedly, I told her that I wasn't comfortable with that. I was terrified of the media hassling my family and me. "No problem", I was told; Avril would get a publication ban but it would only last until the trial began. Avril assured me that even though the media would know my name, they wouldn't be able to do anything with it until the ban was lifted. Even though the trial was years away, I was worried about what it would mean for my family. Once my name was released to the public and the rest of the media, *everyone* would know who I was. I knew there was no such thing as a local story anymore, and I worried what the future would bring. After all, macabre gossip spreads faster than wildfire! However, knowing it was an exercise in futility, I tried my best not to worry about the future.

Avril was kind enough to take the time to explain the law to me, as it related to my case. The law states,
Under Canada's assault law, Quoting Criminal Code, Section 268: 268. (1) Every one commits an aggravated assault who wounds, maims, disfigures or endangers the life of the complainant. (2) Everyone who commits an aggravated assault is guilty of an indictable offence and liable to imprisonment for a term not exceeding fourteen years.
Section 239. (1) Every person who attempts by any means to commit murder is guilty of an indictable offence and liable (a) if a restricted firearm or prohibited firearm is used in the commission of the offence or if any firearm is used in the commission of the offence and the offence v is

committed for the benefit of, at the direction of, or in association with, a criminal organization, to imprisonment for life and to a minimum punishment of imprisonment for a term of (i) in the case of a first offence, five years, and (ii) in the case of a second or subsequent offence, seven years; (a.1) in any other case where a firearm is used in the commission of the offence, to imprisonment for life and to a minimum punishment of imprisonment for a term of four years; and (b) in any other case, to imprisonment for life.

Essentially, even if Twitchell somehow got off on First Degree murder, he would still go to jail for a very long time if charged with my attempted murder.

When I was informed they would be asking to waive the preliminary hearing due to overwhelming evidence for both attempted murder and murder, I was elated. It meant the Crown didn't feel the need to determine whether there was a case, due to an abundance of evidence. I had been given a subpoena to appear for the hearing in September, so I was really happy to hear I would not have to worry about it! I was extremely relieved to learn I would not have to testify for a long while, and it eased my nerves to learn they seemed to have an airtight case against Twitchell.

Before leaving, Avril reminded me I needed to come back to the police station in the near future to watch my video again. She said I would need to have my video testimony sworn on the Bible, in case I died before the case began. A morbid task, I had to make sure the Crown could use my testimony regardless. Finally, they asked me if I would have trouble getting the time off from work in order to attend the trial, and I assured them it would not be a problem. Avril handed me her business card and told me, "If you have any questions at all, call me any time, day or night!" Feeling relieved with the entire exchange, I shook their hands and left the office with Detective Kerr.

I walked back to the police station with Detective Kerr, so we could retrieve my desktop computer. After he signed it out of evidence, we proceeded to go to the Edmonton Police Service labs. Once there, I had to sign a document saying I was okay with them taking my DNA. Since I am not a criminal, I have no problems with them taking my DNA and using it however they needed. The lab tech put on latex gloves and pricked my finger with a pin like tool, and then he rolled my finger onto a piece of paper. It was similar to the paper they use when they take fingerprints, but instead of ink, this was with my own blood. A finger print is like a personal signature and according to legend, one pricked their finger and signed their name in blood when one was signing a pact with the devil. Considering they would be using my DNA to see if it matched some of the blood they found, I felt as if I were signing a pact to incarcerate the devil, for twenty-five to life! I watched as my finger pressed the paper, rolling over my blood in a smear of red. Noticing he didn't have enough blood, the lab technician had to pinprick another finger in order to finish the process and more of my blood was smeared onto the paper. The test complete; I was told to wash my hands in the sink and was given band aids for my tiny wounds.

Finally "free to go," I grabbed my computer and walked out of the police station with Detective Kerr. Before saying goodbye he reminded once again that I would need to come back and watch my taped interview so it could be sworn into testimony. Kerr said that they would probably call me back within a week so I could swear that it was "nothing but the truth, so help me God". On the drive back home, the entire way those words I had heard so many times rang in my ears, "Do you know how lucky you are to be alive?"

Surprisingly, it took several months for me to hear back from the police about my interview being sworn into testimony, not a week like Detective Kerr had assumed. It wasn't until September 2009 that I received a whirlwind of calls from the Edmonton Police Service (EPS) saying they needed me to come in as soon as possible to review my video testimony. After some phone tag, I finally spoke to Detective Dale Johnson, who scheduled a meeting for me to meet with him on September 22, 2009 at 2:00 PM. When the day came, I parked in the Police parking lot, as per Detective Kerr's directions. I was really becoming more and more comfortable with the idea of coming to the Police station and speaking with Homicide Detectives. Since he didn't give me his cell phone number, I went straight to the counter and said, "I have a meeting with Detective Johnson." After the Officer made the call he gave me a blue and white visitor sticker and I got a seat on one of the waiting room chairs while I put the sticker onto my jacket just above my heart.

After about five minutes, Detective Johnson walked through the doors and shook my hand. Thanking me for coming, he walked me through the main security doors so we could go up the elevator to the third floor. After entering the Homicide Division, he directed me to room Number One. Almost a year ago, I had told the entire story to Detective Clark in that very room. Re-watching the video was like reliving the attack for the hundredth time. After I was finished watching the video, I had to force myself back to the present moment. The last time I was there, I "signed" my name in blood but this time I had to swear on the Bible. Whether good or evil was to prevail, that was yet to be determined!

It wasn't until the beginning of March 2011 when a woman by the name of Pat Sharp made several attempts to find me at home. Pat was the Edmonton Police Service witness coordinator and she needed to serve me my subpoena before the trial began, and it was happening soon. The first attempt was made on March 8, 2011. I came home from work and found Pat's business card attached to my front door. On the back was a message saying I needed to get a hold of her as soon as possible. When I called, we arranged for her to deliver the subpoena to me at 1:00 PM on March 14, 2011—five days later. I would be working until 4:00 AM on that morning, so it was going to be very hard for me to wake up that early, but I also knew this was even more important than sleep!

When Pat handed me the subpoena, I noticed that I was witness number 41 and I would be testifying at 9:30 AM on April 1, 2011. It was only two weeks from then! I was unprepared for the news that I would be taking the stand that soon. Reading the document in full, I noticed the address of the Law Courts Building, the name of the accused, Mark Andrew Twitchell, and the victim, Johnny Altinger. It wasn't lost on me that my name could have been where John's was, or even next to his. I held the document in my hands until they were numb, unaware my mind had drifted back to the day and the incident. I put the document away and tried to think of something else.

A few days later, Detective Bill Clark came to visit me at the casino where I worked. A tall, rugged, imposing figure, he shook my hand and asked me how I was doing and when I would be in court. In retrospect, he probably knew when I was testifying; most detectives know the answers to the questions they asked. He was probably making sure I knew and trying to gauge my nervousness. I admitted my nerves were getting the best of me lately and he attempted to ease my concerns. He gave me a few general tips but the most important thing he said was, "just relax and tell everybody your story exactly the way you told me back in 2008." He went on to say, "your story sent chills down my back during that initial interview and that is exactly what they need to hear in court." At least I wasn't the only one with chills running down their spine in this case!

When we were done talking about my concerns, Clark told me he had been approached by *Dateline NBC*. Apparently they and several other news organizations had expressed interest in interviewing me. Detective Clark had been repeatedly asked if I would be interested in doing interviews and asked me if I was interested. Looking back, it may have been another test to see if I would consider violating the publication ban, given all of the media interest. At the time, I merely said, I would consider it after the trial was over and Clark said he would let them know. Detective Clark always made me feel like a friend, ensuring

I was comfortable with everything and knowing I would be nervous. After our chat, he offered to drive and walk me to the courthouse on the first day of April and I gratefully accepted his offer.

Three days after Detective Clark came to visit me, I was contacted by Cheryl Gillan, the paralegal working with the Crown Prosecutors. She left me a voicemail saying I had to schedule a date to come in and meet with Avril and Lawrence to watch my Police interviews, yet again. This time it was so I could remember what I said, since I had already sworn it was true. I agreed to be there on March 28, 2011 at 12:45 PM, for a 1:00 PM meeting. The rule of law appeared to be "cover your ass, just in case."

Later that same day, I received a call from Victim Services. Lili, the same woman who had tried to get ahold of me two and half years earlier, was now looking for me again. For some reason, I recognized her name and voice, despite all the years that had passed. When she first called, I wasn't ready to talk to anyone. I had my own way of dealing with things, and I felt I could handle it; I didn't think talking to anyone about it would help me any more than writing it all down. However, the closer the trial got, the more nervous I became. I started to rethink my need to talk to someone about it all and ended up deciding that it wouldn't hurt to meet with them now. When I called Lili back she said she was glad to finally get a hold of me. She said they needed to know if I would be interested in coming down and filling out a victim impact statement. I asked her why it was necessary and she explained that the victim impact statements would be read at Twitchell's trial and could help with the sentencing. That was all I needed to hear! I agreed to write something down and then asked if they could go through the court proceedings with me. I told her I was getting very nervous about testifying and I needed someone to talk to about it. Although Lili agreed, she warned me that since the trial was underway, they could no longer discuss anything specific to the case. Since Lili said she could go over my general concerns, I decided that something was better than nothing. She checked her schedule and the only time she had available to meet with me was the same day in March that I had a meeting with the Crown. I had to work that day until 4:00 AM, my meeting with the Prosecutors was at 1:00 PM, and I agreed to see her at 8:00 PM. It was then or never, since I would be giving my testimony just four days later.

My very busy day on March 28 seemed to come very quickly. I made my way down to the John E. Brownlee building for my 1:00 PM appointment with the Crown. Just I was exiting the elevator I ran into Crown Prosecutor Lawrence Van Dyke. He remembered me immediately, and showed me the way. Avril wanted to speak with me before I reviewed my video, knowing I would be very nervous. Obviously, murder trials can be especially trying on a person. After getting a few mundane but important details out of the way, like where family could sit, what I should wear and how I would get to the courthouse, I was told I needed to review the video to refresh my memory about what I told them back in 2008.

I exited her office and went to talk to Cheryl to review my video. I was shown to an office that was set up with a laptop and external speakers on the desk. She then put in the DVD into the laptop and pressed play. She left the office and closed the door for privacy and I began watching the first interview I had with the Edmonton Police Service. This was the interview that Detective Clark, rugged Homicide Detective, said gave him chills down his spine. I braced myself to watch it for what seemed like the hundredth time since I had watched it in my head ever since.

I had been keeping up to date with everything happening in the trial before and after my testimony. I even created a scrapbook of the whole trial from all the paper clippings. I couldn't be in court before taking the stand, but I could read the paper since I wasn't part of a sequestered jury. The law keeping me out of the courtroom before my testimony is there to ensure I didn't hear something that could possibly alter my future testimony. Really, it didn't bother me that I couldn't be there until after it was my time to testify since I was already so nervous about having to take the stand in a first degree murder trial. In Canada, there is no death penalty, so at least there wasn't a political side to the trial, as so often is the case in countries like the U.S. where some states execute their worst criminals.

Chapter 3: Before It All

In the summer of 2008, I felt extremely isolated and alone. That year, being single seemed like the end of the world. I was in an unfamiliar city, I was newly separated, and had yet to make many friends. At 33, I often felt like it might be too late for me to start all over again. Although I knew I was still relatively young, it seemed impossible to find love again. Late at night, I lay awake worrying about having to meet new women. I knew dating would be a challenge after being together with the same woman for six years, but part of me assumed it was like riding a bike. My friend and co-worker, Lynn, had introduced me to my ex-wife, Pamela, in 2002, keeping me out of the dating pool until our separation in 2008. In 2003, Pamela and I decided to buy a hair salon together. She was a hair stylist and ran her own business back in Wynyard, Saskatchewan. We made a great team since she worked in the business and I did the accounting, marketing and web design. Our hair salon soon became very prosperous.

The beginning of the end seemed to be in 2005 when Pamela and I moved from Regina, Saskatchewan to Kelowna, B.C. to run a stucco company. The owner lived in Regina and needed managers to be onsite. Seeing how successful our hair salon was, he assumed that success could translate to any industry, no matter how dissimilar.

Unfortunately, the company went under in just a few months. Pamela and I were both forced to find other work in a new city, but she found three jobs in no time at all. I had a diploma in Computer Information Systems and I was finding it difficult to discover a job in my chosen field of study. I remained on unemployment for several months while I looked for a career, but I finally took a job with a security company, to help ease our financial burden. I started working for the Commissionaires, a company that offers non-core police services to more than eighty Canadian municipalities and police departments. They had gotten a contract to secure the grounds of a resort outside of Kelowna while it was being built and I was assigned there. After a few months working for the Commissionaires, I finally left for a job in computers, but when that job wasn't bringing in enough money on its own, I was forced to get a second, part-time job working in a casino doing security. With my two jobs and my wife's three jobs, we didn't see one another very often.

One day Pamela decided she had enough of Kelowna, so she found a job in Edmonton, Alberta. While on a trip visiting friends, she was offered a job and took it on a whim. Since it didn't start for a few months, she also took a short term / contract job in New Brunswick for a few months ending when the job in Edmonton began. I stayed in Kelowna working my two jobs and selling the house so that we could move to Edmonton at the same time. Even though we went ahead with the move to Edmonton, the marriage ended shortly afterwards. It took me completely by surprise! In retrospect, I believe my ex-wife was working so much just to keep herself busy and away from "us." I now realize that the stress of the move, coupled with the crumbling business had put additional pressure on our already strained marriage. I had no clue that there was any problem since she didn't give me any indication that there was. Her unexpected decision to leave has left me with some trust issues. I thought I would be spending the rest of my life with her and I had never imagined anything different, until the day she said she was leaving. I always thought that my marriage would be like my parents' relationship. They have been married for over fifty-two years, which I now understand is an unbelievable feat.

After a period of mourning over the relationship, I picked myself up and got back in the dating pool. Having been in a long-term relationship for six years, I had many unanswered questions about dating. I wondered how to meet someone, what to do once we met, and then where we would go. For the first while, I simply tried to meet women at bars, clubs, and parties but I got tired of that whole scene quickly. More than ready to try something completely different, I signed up for online dating. I had signed up in the year before meeting my ex-wife, but I didn't begin actively online dating until that summer of 2008. Until then, I didn't believe online dating could be a feasible way to meet someone. In 2008, it seemed as though meeting people online had just started to become a socially acceptable way to find a date. Despite some reservations, my decision to meet women was based on my belief "what did I have to lose?" For the first time, I began to feel optimistic about starting over. There were many things that appealed to me about using the Internet to find love and ironically, one of those things was a feeling of safety. Also, it wasn't a last resort for me; it was my chosen technique to find the right one. I quickly found a sense of fellowship that doesn't exist anywhere else. And, at the time it felt comforting knowing other people felt just as alone as I did.

I really liked that I had some control in finding the person I could meet online. I was tired of dating someone for a while and then try to make it work just because we were already together. I didn't want to date any more women with few shared interests and little chemistry. Using the Internet, I was able to pick and choose just those women who truly appealed to me. As stated in my online profile, my ideal woman is attractive, fit, intelligent, and loyal with many shared interests and the ability to talk about a variety of subjects.

I tried a couple of sites with little luck before I found a site called "Plenty of Fish" in June of 2008. It amazed me that one could sign up for free, since I saw some pretty amazing women using it for the same purpose as me: to find a long-term relationship. After a short while, I decided to put up a profile and I used the username, dr_x. This was a name that I had made up when I was kid, playing video games. I thought it was fitting to continue using it for my online profile. The day I signed up, I spent hours and hours sitting at my desktop computer, just looking through profiles of beautiful women who were my matches. It astonished me how many gorgeous women had the same hobbies, interests, and desires as me, living in my area! Reading profile after profile, I felt hopeful for the first time in a very long time. I didn't realize how quickly that feeling could change!

Chapter 4: April Fools?

On the morning of April 1, 2011, I woke up knowing my testimony was to begin in the First Degree Murder case against Mark Twitchell. April Fool's Day was a fitting day for me to testify in a case about being fooled into believing I had found love. On that April 1, I'd have given anything to wake up to find out it was all a horrific prank! That was just first of many auspicious dates surrounding this case and trial.

After tossing and turning for ages, I finally gave up, getting out of bed more than three hours early. I had picked out my clothing the night before, hoping in vain that it would help me sleep. Feeling like a nervous zombie, I ate breakfast and got ready for my ride, my mind on nothing but the trial. From the bottom up, I wore black dress shoes, black dress pants, a blue dress shirt and a yellow tie. I couldn't help but think about being lucky to be alive and in one piece. Without realizing the macabre metaphor, I looked in the mirror and thought to myself, *"I look pretty sharp."*

The day I was to testify actually felt more like a hybrid of April Fool's Day and Groundhog's Day. The Crown Prosecutor had instilled in me the importance of recalling my testimony as if it happened yesterday. They repeatedly said that I needed to recall that day as if it had happened over and over again, every day since. In many ways, it felt like it had; I saw Twitchell everywhere during the day and at night my nightmares took over. And, I may always remember that day as if it happened yesterday.

On April Fool's Day, one can still get charged with perjury if they tell a lie under oath, even if it's an accidental lie. In reality, I was testifying about the day I gave my statement, not the day of my attack. My statement was given to the police exactly one month after the incident, on November 3, 2008. Even though I have since remembered new details, I could not deviate from my original statement while on the stand. I was able to go over my statement beforehand, but that only helped ease my nerves a little. My nightmares would become reality if I slipped up on the stand causing a murderer to walk freely among us. I knew no one would be safe if that happened, including my family and me.

I tried to relax and told myself I just needed to answer truthfully but nothing could prepare me to be a key witness in a First Degree Murder case. I was extremely nervous about testifying in front of John's mother and the rest of his friends and family. At times I told myself, going forward could have prevented Twitchell from taking John's life. For the most part, I try to avoid beating myself up about it. Worrying about wanting to change our past actions is at best an exercise in futility and at worst, a major cause of stress and illness. Despite my lack of sleep and nervous energy, I would have to speak for John, for myself. I wanted to do everything right so that monster would have to go away for a long time. At least I prayed that was what would happen.

On the day I was to testify, I was really happy that Detective Clark, one of the lead Detectives, had offered to drive me to court. Since Canadian and US press had already expressed an interest in speaking to me, I knew there would be a gaggle of reporters waiting to ambush us.

I even began to worry a little when he wasn't there to pick me up when he said he would be, thinking I would have to face them alone. Very organized and professional in my daily life, I was rarely late. I had to be at the courthouse at 9:30 AM and Detective Clark said he would be at my house at 9:00 AM, so when the big hand hit twelve and he wasn't outside my house, I got worried. I thought about what arriving late would mean in this case; I would be inconveniencing several people including a criminal court judge and a jury full of people. I started to panic, thinking Detective Clark had forgotten. Since I was getting more and more comfortable around homicide detectives, I called his personal cell phone. After a few rings, he answered, "Detective Clark," and upon hearing my unease, he explained that he was just a few minutes away from my house. I breathed a sigh of relief, and felt a little silly for worrying in the first place. By the time I grabbed my jacket and locked my front door, Detective Clark's undercover cruiser was outside of my house.

In retrospect, I had no idea whatsoever of my value to the prosecution team! If I asked them to "transport" me there, they probably would have tried to find a way to do it! I got into the vehicle with my interview transcripts in hand, ready for my April Fool's Groundhog Day to begin.

Once I stopped worrying about getting to the courthouse, I began to worry about being closer to the trial I had dreaded for so long. Detective Clark enquired about my nerves, then assured me that it was natural to be apprehensive in a case like this. After decades of testifying in court, nerves rarely entered into the equation for him anymore, but he admitted to being a bit nervous this time. On the way there, Detective Clark reiterated the need to relax and just tell my story like I had told him that first day in November 2008. We chatted a little as he drove and I kept thinking how lucky I was to have him on my case! His offer to drive had given me one less thing to worry about, and his demeanor was calming.

When we arrived, we parked in the police underground parking, a block from the courthouse. On our way, we stopped at Detective Clark's office cubicle so he could pick up a few things. The moment we exited the main front doors of the Police station, there were three reporters with cameras waiting for us. Detective Clark and I were both surprised they knew we would be coming to the courthouse via the police station. Perhaps they had cameras waiting for us at each exit, just in case. I was glad Detective Clark was there when the cameras swarmed me for the first time in my life. I found it very awkward having reporters and cameras in my face; I felt like a new fish in a bowl in a house full of gawkers. While they swarmed us, I became even more nervous about the trial. Thinking about having to face Mark Twitchell, a shiver went down my spine. It was hard to remember what my life was like before he entered into it.

When Detective Clark and I finally got to the courthouse, it was pandemonium. There were even more reporters with cameras, as well as several onlookers. Even when we entered the courthouse, I was being watched by a different set of eyes. Detective Clark waited off to the side while I went through what felt like international airport customs; I had to take off my jacket, belt, watch and wallet before walking through the metal detector. I had been filmed and x-rayed and stared at. Not used to such scrutiny, I felt violated from all angles. We walked over to the courthouse elevators and exited on the fourth floor. The moment we walked around the corner, even more people confronted us. A lineup of people was forming outside of Courtroom 417 on that day. Along with a sea of strangers, I saw the two women from Victim Services and greeted them. Then we all walked past the lineup of enquiring eyes and directly through the courtroom doors.

After getting through the first set of doors, you had to choose between two more sets of doors. The doors to the left led to the courtroom and the ones on the right led to the waiting area. Detective Clark, the Victims Services women and I headed to the waiting area and sat at a boardroom type table with four chairs. The women from Victim's Services sat down with me and began making small talk. They asked me how I was holding up, and I had to admit that I was extremely nervous. I then handed Lili my Victim Impact Statement. She had almost forgotten about it and was happy that I had brought it in. She then left the room to go drop it off in the courtroom. When she came back she informed me that my Victim Impact Statement would not be used for this trial since we were there for John's murder, but would be read if there was a trial for my attempted murder charge. I was a little disappointed that Twitchell would not hear what I had to say but was okay with the decision. For the next few minutes we just chatted while we waited for the Crown Prosecutors, Avril Inglis and Lawrence Van Dyke, to talk to me before court began. As soon as they got there, Detective Clark left to find a seat in the courtroom. Avril sat directly across from me and asked if I would remember the handcuffs if I saw them, and I told her I would. Next she asked me if I would recognize an aerial view of the garage area including the walking path beside it, but since I didn't know the area very well, I couldn't identify it. Before heading off to court, Avril let me know that someone would come and get me when it was time for me to testify. After that, the women from Victims Services stayed with me, but since my nerves were shot, we did not say much. I was worried about remembering exactly what I told them in 2008, even though I have since remembered and learned new information. I felt uneasy about having to keep my testimony unerringly the same.

That Friday was Day 17 of the trial. After about ten minutes, which felt like three hours, Lawrence opened the door and said it was time. As if the weather knew the case against the devil was beginning, it went from -1 to +2 degrees Celsius at 9:00 that morning. Prosecutor Van Dyke instructed me to follow him until he stopped and then to continue on without him to the witness stand. Walking through the courtroom doors, I noticed the people lining the walls, all standing up for me. After being called into the courtroom, Twitchell looked up, but only for a moment. Feeling like a bride who ended up at a murder trial by mistake, I walked up the aisle with Lawrence. All those eyes on me, I continued to follow Lawrence until he went to stand beside Avril. Just like the father giving away the Bride, I continued on to the witness stand by myself. Standing alone beside the Judge's desk, I felt sick looking out at all of the people who were there to hear what I had to say. Would I be the one to put the nail in the coffin? The entire room so silent, I was sure everyone could hear my fast shallow breathing.

Judge Clackson was on my left and twelve jurors stood up to the right of me, and it all felt surreal. Prosecutors, Avril and Lawrence stood directly in front of me and looking to the left, I saw Mark Twitchell. He was standing beside his defense attorney and for the first time since the night he tried to kill me, I stood before him hoping in vain he would make eye contact. A coward until the end, he kept his head down and would not return my gaze. On the day I was to testify, Twtichell was wearing glasses, which threw me because he looked different to than my memory of him. Later I found out that just prior to my entrance, he was seen laughing with his attorney, so it didn't seem as if he was close to as nervous as I was at that moment.

The judge gave everyone permission to sit down, except me. I would have to stand the entire time, as is the procedure in Canadian legal cases. Now everybody could get a really good look at me, adding to my apprehension. The bailiff asked me to pick up the Bible next to me and put my right hand on it. Then the bailiff said, "Do you swear or affirm to tell the truth... under penalty of perjury?"

"I do." I said, marrying me to whatever I said from that moment on. I looked at the sea of silent faces, and tensely waited. Looking at Twitchell, I still wasn't able to make him return my gaze.

Before long, Judge Clackson addressed the jurors, saying, "You are entitled to hear if the diary is factual. I ask you to consider Mr. Tetreault's evidence in writing. You cannot use this evidence to convict Mr. Twitchell for Mr. Altinger's murder." Before Avril began asking me questions she started by putting up pictures of the garage site on the projection screen. Bringing me back to that day, she asked about my life at the time of the incident. I replied, "I was living in Edmonton, working for Sapphire Technologies on contract for a few months and I was working part-time for a casino. I lived on the northeast side. I was a member of the Plenty of Fish site. It was free, I didn't pay."

"In September of 2008 you saw photos of a pretty girl, can you describe her?"

Taking a deep breath, I steadied myself and replied,

"She was blonde, fairly attractive, five-foot-six…" I said, thinking that after everything that happened, "Spiderwebzz" was the perfect name for Sheena! Instead of a web spun by a spider to trap insect prey, it was a web of lies spun in a garage by a man to trap his prey. Next, Avril showed me a picture of the woman known as "Sheena" so I could identify her as the woman presented to me, and I did so.

As for Twitchell, he was all alone in court. Although his parents and sister were allowed to attend, they never appeared once. His infamous diary, *SKConfessions* (Serial Killer Confessions), which was recovered from his computer, is eerily similar to my report of the incident. It was read aloud to the courtroom and the jury by Constable Michael Roszko of the Edmonton Police Service's Technological Crime Unit on Day 13 of the Trial. The number 13 has always been known to be an unlucky number. I hoped that these ominous coincidences would amount to nothing more than that. Had I been superstitious, my nerves would have likely transformed into panic.

As I was to describe how I picked "him," Twitchell's diary describes how he chose me, coldly writing of his preparation in setting his trap for me.

When I come across a single man in his late thirties to early forties who is self-employed, lives alone and stands between 5'7 and 5'11 with an average body type weighing in between 150 and 180 lbs., I know I've found my ideal target.

Such was the case with a man I will refer to as Frank. That of course is not his real name and I won't divulge any other sensitive details about the situation but Frank was my very first target ever. I roped him in with a profile I was quite proud of featuring photos of a blonde I would like to bang myself.

Chapter 5: There She Was

"Spiderwebzz" was a beautiful "girl-next-door" type with undeniable sex appeal. She was average height with blonde hair and big blue eyes.* Her profile stood out, and I immediately knew I had to find out more! She had three pictures attached, each more appealing than the last. Skimming through her profile, our common ground made me take a second look. She wrote that she was looking to meet new people because she just moved to Edmonton from Alberta's neighboring province to the west, British Columbia. Not only were we both in new cities, we both had moved to Edmonton after living in British Columbia for the last three years.

*Spkerwebzz aka Sheena aka Mark

Gilles Tetreault

While I was looking at "Spiderwebzz"'s profile, I noticed she had come online at the same time. Feeling like we might have a connection, I made the decision to send her an instant message. She replied immediately. She was very natural, engaging, intelligent, and flirtatious and we seemed to hit it off right away! After a few messages, she revealed to me that her real name was "Sheena." She said she lived in the south central part of Edmonton in the electoral district known as Millwoods. I was happy that she seemed forthcoming with her personal information so quickly. She was far more forthcoming than most women I had met. She inquired into my plans for the upcoming weekend and I took it as a cue to ask her out. I wrote that I didn't have anything planned. She then wrote back to me asking if I would like to meet up that Friday, October 3, 2008. After a few nervous heartbeats, I eagerly accepted. I waited for what seemed like an eternity for a response, and then she merely wrote, "I'll think about it". Worried I misread her and came on too strong when accepting her invitation, I waited impatiently for her next message. After a few more worrisome minutes thinking I had blown my chances, she sent another message suggesting we go to dinner and a movie. At that point, I was happy to agree to anything she wanted to do!

Sheena told me that she liked to go to dinner before going to a movie so she could avoid all of the junk food theatres serve. She suggested we go to Joey's Global Grill & Lounge restaurant in Edmonton's South Common Mall before heading to the nearby Cineplex Odeon movie theatre. She also chose the movie, *Nick & Norah's Infinite Playlist*, which I assumed was a chick flick since I had never heard of it. When she told me I would need to pick her up at 7:00 PM on Friday night, I was too happy to do anything but agree. I didn't care what we did or where we went, and I was more than happy she chose the what, where and when. I have always liked a confident woman who knows what she wants.

I was so excited to have plans with her that even her strange instructions didn't put me off. To get to her basement apartment door, at the back of the house, I had to go through the detached garage. She said it was the only way and gave several reasons. There was a no parking zone in front of the house and a bus stop on the opposite side of the street. The only way to get to her basement apartment, at the back of the house, was via the backyard.

Unfortunately she said, the fence was padlocked, preventing any pedestrian access from the alleyway. I was told that the only way to get into the backyard was to through the detached garage. She said she would leave one of the bay doors partly open so that I could make my way through the garage and exit out the pedestrian door on the other side. From there, all I had to do was walk across the backyard and knock on the basement apartment door. Assuring me it was the only way, she began to end our chat. Before saying goodbye, she reminded me to let her know what road I would be taking so that she could send me proper directions. Excited at the prospect of meeting someone so interesting and beautiful, I emailed her later that night to say just that.

Outgoing and personable, I rarely hesitate when communicating my opinions and expectations to people. The next day I couldn't wait to get home from work so I could check my messages. On that Tuesday night, my

Internet browser seemed to take forever to open. I logged on to the dating side, since it had been our only method of communication. And when I saw her reply, I began smiling widely. I was happy to see she seemed as excited as I was to continue our conversation. She provided directions as promised, but parts were in great detail and other parts were vague or nonsensical. Although somewhat confusing, I figured she had merely misread Fort Road for Groat Road and I didn't think much of it. This is the actual message she sent me with the directions to her place:

So ok, Friday. If you're coming from the North on Groat, get on Calgary trail and when you get to the South side and jump on Whitemud. Then go south on 50 St. Take a right on 40 Avenue and after a block or two take the very first right into the alley. It's marked by a yellow crosswalk sign so pay attention. Then go left and pull in to the only driveway on your left that isn't paved. lol. Seriously, who ever heard of a driveway that looks like the Amazon? Whatever, it won't swallow your car, I promise. There's some garbage up against the fence like an old couch and such but it might be gone by Friday, who knows. Like I said, the garage door will be open for you a touch. Don't worry about neighbors thinking you're a burglar. Everyone knows there's nothing valuable in there . . . except my car of course, oi.

See you then.
Sheena

I found it odd that she didn't give me an actual house number, or even a phone number I could call in case I got lost. I emailed her requesting more information, wanting to clarify which door I should knock on. I also wanted to make sure I *had* to go through the garage to get to the backyard. As I communicated all of these issues to her, I hoped I wouldn't come across as high-maintenance. Fortunately, she did reappear, but sadly her message did nothing to quell my concerns about getting there. She merely wrote,

"Yeah first visible back door coming out of the garage, knock away."

Frustrated with her ignoring my requests, I wrote back to her saying, "At least give me your phone number, in case I get lost." I didn't see the harm in asking for it, but I hit another brick wall. Sheena told me she refused to give out her street address or her phone number, for "safety reasons". Confused, I couldn't understand why she was okay with giving me perfect directions, but not the address. Sensing my frustration, Sheena promised to give me her phone number *if* the date went well on Friday. At that point, I didn't want to give her any reason to change her mind, so I left it alone. Even though I had concerns, I was mostly focused on how happy I would be when we finally did meet!

The next day, I awoke feeling just as frustrated with the lack of information Sheena was willing to provide. Mostly, my concerns were around making sure everything went well on the date. So, I sent a message saying, "If I don't show up, it's because I couldn't find your place." Although it sounds that way, I wasn't trying to be passive aggressive. I honestly wanted her to convey to her that I would never bail on her on purpose. I also reiterated how excited I was about our date and told her I thought we would have a great time. In her response, she made a feeble attempt to reassure me. Her message said,

"There's certainly no other driveways along our alley like this one and the half open car door is a dead give away. lol See you 7 on Friday."

At that point, I let it go. Despite the uncertainty I was feeling, I thought it might be worth it to get the chance to meet her. For the most part, I was pretty confident that I would finally meet someone worth getting to know better. I was fairly sure I would find the place.

Admittedly, part of me was hoping that her forward nature might mean the date might go further than just dinner and a movie! Any guy would have to admit they would at least *hope* for that. I was almost positive the night would end well. At the very least, I was sure I would get another date. I couldn`t have been more wrong about everything!

Chapter 6: Forward?

"Was she forward?" the Prosecutor asked.

"Yes." I responded. Thinking back to our conversations, I should have known that she had been advancing too quickly. I guess you could say she was inconsistently forward, giving me detailed directions, but no address or phone number. At the time, I didn't listen to my instinct telling me something wasn't quite right. I continued to respond to Avril's question saying, "She asked me immediately what I was doing the following Friday. I asked her if she wanted to go out. We agreed to go out to dinner at Joey's and to go to the movies after." Then I told her about how the date was her idea and that our only form of conversation had been on the dating website; we never spoke on the phone or emailed.

"Can you please read aloud the message she gave you with the directions to the garage?" Avril asked. I read "Sheena's" directions for the court and to a persistently indifferent Twitchell. Later I would learn that he was writing a speech on his notepad using an alien language from Star Wars that uses figures to represent letters in the alphabet. A true psychopath, Mark seemed to be more concerned with himself and his time in the spotlight, and he was fantastic at acting like he was engaged and interested.

I continued to testify to the rest of the courtroom full of strangers. I spoke to the judge, the jury, and Avril. Everyone except Twitchell was captivated with what I had to say. I couldn't help but think that the reporters and jurors had read a copy of *SKConfessions* and were already seeing the similarities with my story, just as the homicide detectives had their copies while they were watching me give my first testimony to Detective Clark, all those years ago. They could essentially read along with Twitchell's account. I testified that, "I kept asking for her street address, phone number, anything but she kept giving me excuses. I understood because there are a lot of stalkers out there, but I thought it odd that she didn't give me her house address."

Pretending he was actually creative, Twitchell's "diary" was merely a rehashing of events. Like my testimony, *SKConfessions* speaks of his intent to confuse his address. It also talks about his intentions for me:

I asked him to pick me up from my residence at a prescribed time on a particular night of the week and then gave him detailed instructions on how to find the place. I gave him some song and dance routine about how my landlord had the property set up to where the back gate was broken and padlocked and there was nowhere in front to park because of a no parking zone and a bus stop across the street. So I told him I would leave the garage door open for him to come in through and then to come back door of the house, all the while realizing, of course that he would never make it that far. So the message was received and confirmed, and I waited.

Chapter 7: Excited Anticipation

When Friday's date with Sheena finally came around, I didn't even feel like going to work! An easy going and social person, I was far more excited than nervous. At the time I was doing computer technical support out of Edmonton's downtown core. Most days I enjoyed my work and my coworkers. On that Friday, I couldn't wait for the workday to finish. I could barely concentrate on anything but the date, but I didn't let on. I was professional in the office and rarely talked about my personal life.

Before the end of the workday, some of my co-workers invited me to go to a pub and have a couple of drinks. I was caught a bit off guard because normally I would have felt an obligation to go. Instead I told them I had other plans because no man in his right mind would have bailed on a date with a beautiful woman, just to have drinks with the people he saw almost every day! For some reason, I didn't tell them I had a date. It was as if I knew I wouldn't want them to know about the night for some reason.

Upon exiting the office, I realized that I would never make it in time. For some reason, even though I knew I wouldn't be able to leave work until 6:00 PM, I had foolishly agreed to pick her up at 7:00 PM. I knew there was no way I would be able to drive all the way home, change, and then make it to the other side of the city in an hour! I hoped if I just drove fast, I might be able to pick her up in time. I didn`t want to ruin the date by being too late to have dinner before the movie. The last thing I wanted was to make a bad first impression! When I got into my truck, all I could think was, "HURRY!"

Even though I drove as fast as humanly possible, I didn`t pull into my driveway until 6:22 PM. Wanting to look casual, I picked out a short sleeve buttoned up black shirt, coupled with a pair of blue jeans and comfortable yet fashionable slip-on shoes. I noticed my hair was a mess so I added some water and gel and hoped for the best. Before leaving I grabbed my wallet and my cell phone. I put the cell phone onto my belt clip and my wallet in my back pocket. Since I didn't have any cash, I was carrying my debit and credit cards. Before heading out the door I made the last minute decision to throw on a light black summer jacket. It was unseasonably warm for an October evening in Edmonton but I knew it would probably get a lot cooler at night. I had no idea how significant that last minute decision would be. Throwing on a jacket may have saved me from a lot more than a cold that night!

I checked the time on the dashboard clock of my black 1998 Ford Ranger and it read 6:45 PM. I had no way to call Sheena to say that I would be late, and there was no time to go back inside to log onto my computer. This was exactly why I had wanted to know her phone number. To be there by 7:00 PM, I had to do my best to get there as quickly as possible.

I drove away feeling excited that I would soon be on a date with a beautiful, intelligent, confident woman. I thoroughly followed the directions that Sheena provided for me. My landmark was a yellow crosswalk sign, advising motorists the need to yield to pedestrians. Throwing caution to the wind, I took a right down the alleyway. I continued driving very slowly as the path curved to the left, looking for the white garage with two faded yellow garage doors. As directed, it was on the left side of the alleyway.* I knew I was at the right place when I saw the garage door on the right side was partially open. At last, I had arrived!

The actual garage, after the investigation had begun.

Once I changed her directions to include Fort Road instead of Groat Road, I didn't have any difficulty finding the right place. As I parked my truck I noticed the garbage and old couch up against the fence. Even though she had mentioned that stuff might still be there by Friday, it felt odd to me. It didn't make sense that anyone could leave it out for that long without someone else picking it up! I parked in front of the open garage door, my headlights facing it. I was able to leave about ten feet between the garage door and the front of my truck without sticking out into the alleyway.

A quick glance at the clock on my truck's dashboard told me I had arrived at 7:15 PM. Since I was late, it added to my sense of urgency, causing me to rush. I really hoped she wouldn't be too upset about my tardiness and decide to cancel our date or hold it against me in some other way. I locked my truck and then rushed toward the partially open garage door, which was automatic and rolled directly up. Even though I'm five feet, seven inches tall, I only had to squat down a little to get in.

I looked into the garage for a few seconds and nothing seemed out of the ordinary; a quick glance in dim light while in a hurry and it seemed to be just like any other residential garage. I remember it being very dirty inside with a few shelving units and seeing the windows covered with some type of dark film. An old wooden chair and a steel barrel were in the right hand corner of the garage as well but not much else. In retrospect, I only saw what I expected to see. In reality, I missed a green tarp that covered most of the left side of garage, and everything that lay behind it.

Adjusting my eyes to the light, my only thought was finding the door leading to the backyard, and her basement apartment. When I saw the pedestrian door at the back left corner of the garage, I headed towards it. In a hurry to meet my date, I felt excited to finally be there. All I was thinking about was what might happen that night. Not once did I wonder why her car wasn't in the garage, even though she said it was the "one valuable thing she kept in there". I made it all the way to the door, and even grabbed the doorknob, but I never got a chance to turn it.

As soon as I got to the door, someone grabbed me from behind! I thought it might be Sheena playing a joke, until the grip tightened beyond what any average woman could muster. Before I knew it, my attacker landed multiple blows to the back of my head and started prodding my chest with some kind of a black tool that made a loud eerie noise and sparked bright blue when he pressed the trigger. I moved to the right to try to get out of harm's way but got stuck between two wooden shelving units. When I was finally able to turn my head to see who was attacking me, what I saw sent chills down my spine!

The first thing I noticed was a black and gold painted hockey mask.* I felt as if the wind was knocked out of my sails; I had been set up and there would be no date! The next thing I noticed was the hoodie that covered his entire head. All that kept running through my head was, "Who was this man attacking me?"

The actual mask

My first thought was that he was going to mug me. Thinking that, I knew to remain calm. At that moment, I thought that the worst case scenario would mean giving him my wallet and truck keys and hoping he would let me go. I knew that I had to be smart about every move. Suddenly, I thought of a plan to escape; a glimmer of hope, I now had a strategy to get away! The problem was, I wasn't sure how I was to going to implement my plan.

As I struggled to get out of his grasp, he continued prodding me with his black tool. I wiggled my way out of his clutches and started to move around the garage towards the open garage door, but as soon as I would try to make my way a bit closer to the open garage door, the masked man would prod me with what I found out later to be a stun baton again and again.

Finally I started to get frustrated with his useless weapon, so I grabbed the end of the baton with my left hand, pushing it away from me. Unfettered by this, he kept pressing the trigger, zapping my bare hand. It did not hurt, and I gave him a look that said, "I'm not impressed with your weapon".

Seeing that the stun baton wasn't doing what he intended, he pulled it away from my grasp. Without seeing how, I noticed he had gotten it back onto his belt. As soon as I tried going toward the pedestrian door at the back of the garage, he would block my way. At this point we were quite far apart and still facing one another.

When he realized that I wasn't going to abide him, he pulled out a handgun. The barrel was pointed at me and I knew in that moment that I had to do what he said. I had to assume the gun was real, and I acted accordingly. If it was a real gun, I wasn't sure if I would be getting out alive. I also knew that I couldn't just go down like this!

He kept the gun pointed at me and speaking in an authoritative voice, he said, "Get down on the ground, lie down on your stomach, put your head down, and put your arms behind your back!" Even though it was still light out, it was now considerably darker in the garage. I wasn't close enough to see if the gun was real and I knew that there was no way out if it was. Since I wasn't sure whether the weapon was real or not, I had no other option than to comply with the gunman's orders. With a masked man watching my every move, I slowly got down to the ground.

As commanded, I got onto my stomach, put my forehead on the floor and lastly, my arms behind my back. I decided that if this was a mugging then I would let him have everything I had, and told him so. As long as he let me go, he could have everything, and I wouldn't tell anyone, I said. At this point, I was willing to say everything he wanted to hear so he would let me go and he was willing to say anything I wanted to hear to keep me there with as little hassle as possible. He tried to assure me if I co-operated, I wouldn't get hurt.

But, I wasn't about to make things easy for him, so I kept disobeying his orders. I kept looking up so I could see what he was doing. Every time he noticed me looking, he yelled at me to put my head back down. I glanced back up and saw him taking out some grey duct tape. That was when I realized it wasn't just an ordinary mugging! When he noticed my head was up again he yelled, "Put your head down and close your eyes!" Not wanting to push my luck, I kept my head down and I didn't see how he was able to rip a piece of tape off the roll while still holding the gun.

The next thing I knew, tape was covering my eyes! Not only was this not a mugging, he planned on killing me! Without the ability to see anything he was doing, I began to tear up. Then I heard a jiggling noise and couldn't help but think that it was coming from his belt. That's when I assumed the worst and thought he was also going to rape or kill me! I had my hands behind my back and in a few moments he was going to tape them up, leaving me with very few options. Tears streamed down my face and onto the cold garage floor.

Chapter 8: Backward

As Crown Prosecutor Avril Ingles was having me identify the garage I had been attacked in, I thought back to that night. One by one, I testified that it was, in fact, the garage and I couldn't help but go back to how I felt when I first realized I was being attacked. I had to admit that I didn't notice everything in the garage that I was now seeing in the exhibits Avril was showing me. I testified, "I didn't look around much because I was late and was rushing." Remembering that night, I said, "I was focused to get to the door to get to the house. I did see things covering the windows but I can't remember what it was." I tried to explain, "It was still light out but inside the garage it was dark."

"Was there enough light to read text?" Avril asked, trying to convey to the jurors how dark it was.

"No." I said, trying to recreate the scene in as much detail as possible. I couldn't help but keep thinking of all of the things I did wrong, and all the things I did right. Avril gently prompted me to keep going. It was difficult retelling everything in front of the captivated masses and emotionless Twitchell. When I was in that garage, not once did I see the green sheet or the plastic sheeting coating the walls and floors in what was now known as the "Kill Room." A chill went down my spine thinking about what happened in that garage.

I tried to focus on giving Avril my testimony, so I continued, "I went towards the door…I didn't even get to turn the knob when someone tagged me from behind. It felt like a bear hug. I thought it was Sheena maybe playing a joke. I turned around and all of a sudden I saw a man with a hockey mask!" Then I said that I knew it wasn't a date at that point and that "I thought I was getting mugged!"

Next I was asked to describe the hockey mask. I told them it had a visible cut up around the mouth and that I didn't remember the color. When asked how I was able to identify that mask as being the one I saw that night, I said, "But once I saw the picture on the Internet later, it all came back and I immediately recognized it."

"Is this the mask you saw?" Avril asked, showing me an exhibit with a picture showing the mask found in Twitchell's home basement. I knew it was the same mask he wore the night he attacked me. It was also the mask he wore the night he attacked John, according to DNA evidence. "Yes." I said, going right back to the first time I saw it. Another chill went down my spine as I looked at the top of Twitchell's head, but he looked like he couldn't be less interested. I continued telling my story, "From that point I knew I had to escape somehow. I had a plan but I had to put it into place. I saw a black object that made some really loud noise and it looked blue." It was the stun baton that didn't work according to plan, I said, "It didn't really hurt me at all, but the person was placing it all over my chest." I told the court we were moving around the garage until we got to a standstill, "We were just standing there looking at each other." I told them, shrugging, "I looked at him like hey this isn't hurting me."

I told the court about trying to get to the pedestrian door, but not getting to it in time. He got in my way and then I saw the handgun and had to abide his orders, "He yelled 'get down on the ground, put your head down and put your hands behind your back!'" I began to flash back to the feeling of the cold garage floor beneath my outstretched body, and unable to keep my composure any longer. I finally began to tear up right there on the stand. It was the last thing I wanted to do but my emotions were raw standing in front of a disinterested Twitchell.

Avril asked if I was okay to continue and I said that I was, giving her a little smile showing that I had regained my composure. Then, I continued, "A lot of things went through my head, you know the way it does, everything flashing before you. I saw pictures of my family and my life…" I continued to tell the court about my life flashing before my eyes.

Twitchell's script for his short film, *House of Cards,* wasn't read in court. If it had been, everyone would have known that he wrote about everything beforehand also, saying, "He's about seven steps from the door when the unmistakable sound of a stun baton being fired explodes from the darkness." He planned it out, acted it out, and then actually did it! Once again, Twitchell's diary was identical to my description of the garage and my attempted murder. He admits to removing the address from the back of the garage so that no one would be able to have more than directions. He coldly wrote about me as if he were hunting an animal instead of another human being:

I took two swift silent steps toward my target and pressing the baton across the back of his neck, pulled the trigger. It shocked and jumped but did little more than merely alert the bastard to what was really going on. It did not render his muscles unusable and the little shit fought back.

I had a distinct advantage. I was taller and outclassed him in tenacity and strength. This was also my environment and he wasn't expecting to run into a psycho in a mask, only a beautiful woman he hoped he would get lucky with. The confusion played to my benefit and I struck him repeatedly. He yelled "what the fuck" at the top of his lungs. The noise was something I had hoped to avoid but I paid it no mind and continued attempting to subdue this defiant little shit.

I dropped the baton and punched him several times in the side of the head but still he would not go down. He broke free and I could tell he would make for the door, for the way he came in so I reached into my pocket and withdrew the gun.

I pointed it straight at him and all of a sudden he took me seriously, his eyes wide. I commanded him to get down on the floor, to which he obeyed quickly. If he lifted his head even the slightest bit I warned him against it. I removed my gloves and went for the duct tape. I tore a piece off and slipped it over his eyes.

Chapter 9: Flashing Before

Lying on the garage, tape over my eyes, it's difficult to explain what happened next. Although I had always been a skeptic about these kinds of things, I couldn't deny it was happening. Time slowed down and my entire life was replayed in flash images. The visualizations were very quick pictures of my family without sound. Everything went completely silent while I saw my life flash before my eyes.

I saw everything in slow motion. Events I hadn't thought of in years dominated my consciousness. Images played for me, showing me myself throughout the years. I saw my brother Roger and his family. Lying face down, my eyes covered, my arms behind my back, I saw my mother and father and my birthplace of Gravelbourg, Saskatchewan. I had flashes of myself going to French immersion classes and I saw myself speaking French with my parents.

I never wanted for anything as a child. Everything I could ever need was just a bike ride away. Where I grew up, it was so safe that we didn't have to lock our doors during the day. Most of my best friends were my cousins. My mother's side of the family was so huge that it bred me several lifelong friendships. Given this, it didn't seem to matter that my father's side of the family left me with cousins that either lived too far away or were much older. I was lucky to have grown up with an abundance of homemade best friends!

After grade seven, I had to decide to which high school to go to. I could either go to the public Gravelbourg High School or the College Mathieu, a private French school. I was very lucky that they were both in my hometown. The public High School had all English speaking classes with one hour of French per day and the French school was all in French except for one hour of English per day. The College Mathieu was also very prestigious, attracting students from other provinces who would board right on campus, away from their families, just so they could attend. Also, all of my friends were going there. However, private school comes at a cost so for grade eight I chose to go to the Gravelbourg public High School. Grade eight turned out to be one of the worst times in my life; I had no friends and I felt out of place. My self-esteem dropped and my grades suffered as well. I saw flashes of a sad kid, changing into a much happier kid once grade nine rolled around. That year, I decided to go to the College Mathieu where I had a much better time with my old friends and I met many new friends.

Every aspect of my school life improved in grade nine at the College Mathieu. I saw myself playing on the basketball team, playing point guard. Even though I wasn't the greatest player, I made the team every year and enjoyed the game. I also performed much better academically. Since the French High School was a newer school they had better technology, which was particularly suited to me since I was looking forward to a career in computer sciences.

Growing up, my older brother was my role model. I looked up to him and wanted to be just like him. Partly due to his influence, I set personal goals and was able to achieve them all. I set goals like graduating high school and getting work in the computer field. I watched myself graduating from the Saskatchewan Institute of Applied Science and Technology (SIAST) with a diploma in Computer Information Systems and I was proud of myself.

My best friend growing up was my cousin, Jason. We played together almost every weekend when we were kids. We liked video and board games but we also made our own games. We often played out these games with our Star Wars and Super Powers figures, and our Dukes of Hazard cars. Jason and I went biking all the time and listened to the same music. We often exchanged cassette tapes, which were as good as gold to us back then. We would record each other copies of our newest tapes and records. We also made mix tapes from all of our favourite songs and new ones as they changed. Jason and I were huge fans of Elvis, thanks to my uncle who had a large collection of his music. I grew up listening to Elvis Presley records, and I'm still a huge fan to this day. I had an idyllic childhood full of creativity and wonder and I never wanted for anything. I realize how lucky I am. While I am fortunate I had an incredibly happy childhood, it was surprising how much my past was like the man who would attempt my murder. Unbeknownst to me at the time, Twitchell had a similar childhood to mine. I read about his upbringing after he was arrested. He and I both had great parents, and neither of us suffered any abuse or any great hardships; for us, growing up was nothing short of idyllic. Up until that moment, neither of us had even committed a crime.

Lying there on that garage floor, it flashed before me almost too quickly for me to grasp the magnitude of it all. Little did I know, a week from now the garage floor would be covered in blood.

Chapter 10: By Any Means Necessary

Snapping out of it, I quickly realized that he thought his life was more valuable than mine. Less human than human, he was treating me like a science project. To him I was some "thing" to be used as a learning tool, to be tossed away afterwards. I had no idea that I was literally and figuratively a trial and error "assignment" to him. He had filmed this moment with actors and now he was acting it out for himself in a macabre case of purposeful art imitating life. He did not have a creative bone in his psychotic body.

After seeing my life flash before me, I knew my life was worth fighting for. I was not a "deserving" victim like the character "Dexter" would have chosen to kill. My only crime was being lonely and choosing to do something about it, by any means necessary. I also realized that since I never told anybody where I was going, no one would ever know where I was or what had happened to me. I had not seen his kill tools or the plastic sheeting, but I was fully enraged as I was upon seeing the stun baton and the handgun! In that moment, all I knew was that I needed to survive so I could see my family and friends again. I knew I couldn't go out like that!

I began to clearly focus on what I needed to do to save myself. It wasn't the time to think about what I had done wrong to get myself there. All I had space in my brain for was survival. I decided that if I was going to die, I might as well die my way instead of his, and I wasn't going to lay down and die easy! I had to take the chance and try to fight him off since he had inadvertently given me the chance to. I had become the variable he didn't plan for when the stun baton didn't work, but I knew whatever my next move was, I would have to do it soon. If he tied my hands or feet up with duct tape, it would be over for me because this wasn't a movie. At least not to me; this was a real life horror story and I didn't yet know how it ended.

Lying on the floor in that garage, I suddenly understood I had the advantage. I took a deep breath, and then I moved my arms, disobeying his orders. I ripped the tape off of my eyes, and I then stood up. I first mumbled, "I can't do this," then turned around to face him and then yelled, "SORRY, I CAN'T GO DOWN LIKE THIS!" with tears streaming down my face. I was now ready to fight for my life! The man got very angry and demanded that I get back down on the ground. He didn't yet know that I had decided I would not be following his orders.

He then pulled the gun out and pointed it straight at me once more. I decided that regardless of his weapon, the time was now to act. My only hope was to try and grab ahold of the end of the handgun and steer it away from my body in case it went off. When I got a bit closer to him, I grabbed the barrel of the gun with my left hand, shocking him. Adrenaline pumping, I grabbed and pushed the gun away from my body. The moment I touched the gun's barrel, I realized it was indeed plastic. I had never been so happy and angry at the same time! The attacker had my right arm so I held onto the fake gun with my left hand, and I began trying to bend and break it, but it was still tightly in his grasp. As we struggled, I could feel the gun bending slightly and when this happened, the masked man got very angry and began yelling at me to stop. He wasn't aware that I was no longer afraid of him or of his fake gun anymore. I was fearlessly fighting for the right to see my family again!

With an entirely different attitude and my survival instinct and adrenaline kicking into full gear, we began struggling to reposition ourselves. I continued to try and break the gun until I saw a pair of black, heavy duty metal handcuffs lying on the cement floor. Having worked in Security at a Casino, I knew they weren't a cheap pair of cuffs. Seeing the cuffs set off a burst of emotion. This was sick behavior.

Looking at him differently now, I was fully ready to fight back. I let go of the fake gun and picked up the handcuffs to use them as a weapon. This made the man angry and he yelled at me to put them down. I thought about it and realized I would have to hit him on the back of the head with the cuffs to do any damage, given his mask. So, I threw them into the right hand corner of the garage, where the man wouldn't be able to easily retrieve them. I never really saw where they landed, but there were other items in that corner so I figured it would be harder for him to find them there. I didn't know that I had thrown them near his kill tools.

At this point, I knew the only chance I had was to fight, so I got mentally ready to take on my attacker, despite his bigger size. The masked man came after me and we kept holding each other's arms down like a couple of hockey players on skates. I wanted to punch him in the face but I was unable to since he was indeed wearing a hockey mask. I decided to try punching him in the stomach but for some reason my punch was extremely weak and didn't seem to do anything to him. I couldn't figure out why I was so weak; it felt like a real life horror story, your arms unable to punch your assailant rendering your punches completely ineffective.

At one point I got a little too close to the man, and he caught me off guard, head bunting me. He almost caught me directly in the middle of my forehead and I knew it could have been much worse if he had landed it dead on! I had to be careful not to get too close so I wouldn't get knocked out. I tried kicking him in the mid-section but he moved to the side and he almost caught my leg, grabbing my shoe. I also had to be careful not to lose my shoe since I would need both of them to run away. He then also tried to kick me in the mid-section but I was able to evade. He also came close to knocking me down, which would have probably been game over.

Chapter 11: Groundhog Day

My testimony seemed to go on forever, but at the same time, it was over in an instant. I told Prosecutor Avril Ingles what I did next. I said, "I grabbed the gun with my left hand and felt…it was a plastic gun. I tell my friends this: it was the best feeling in the world!" Smiling widely as I said it.

"Why?" Avril asked me.

"Because, I wasn't afraid of the gun anymore." I replied. The judge smiled and I continued with even more confidence, looking at Twitchell while saying, "I was very angry." Once again I willed him to look at me but he wouldn't. I said, "I really wanted to break that gun so I started prying it." I explained that we were both holding onto the gun while I tried to break it, saying, "It almost seemed like I was bending the gun. We kind of shuffled and switched positions and to my right I see a pair of thick, black metal handcuffs." I looked at Twitchell saying, "When I saw that, I knew it's probably much bigger than a robbery!" Holding my composure, I told the court how I grabbed the handcuffs and threw them into the corner of the garage in a pile of other things, where he couldn't reach them easily.

Next I spoke to Avril, saying that he began talking to me at that point. I told her, "He said that since I wasn't co-operating, 'This is the way it would have to be,' and he began punching me in the side of my head." Then I said, "His first blow hit me on the left side of my face, right below the temple. His punches fueled my anger, and I wanted to see what this guy was really made of!" I took a deep breath and told them I tried to grab for his mask and tried to push it up. I caught a glimpse of his cheek but the mask was on too tight and I wasn't able to pull it off much more. I was also aware that I wasn't able to stay that close to him for fear of getting knocked out. Then I told them that I let him punch me because every time he did I was able to maneuver myself into any position I wanted."

Remembering him hitting me again and again, I flashed back to that garage on Friday October 3, 2008. I was able to retell my story with stunning accuracy, time after time. Every day since the attack, it felt like it happened yesterday. I had the same yesterday over and over again, like a reverse *Groundhog Day*, as if this really were a movie. Talking about the blows I took to the head, I inadvertently touched my left temple where he had done most of the damage.

Twitchell's diary spoke about all of the things *he* did wrong:

> *It was then that I told him that if he did what I told him to, that I would let him live. I brought one arm down around his back and was reaching for the other arm when he began defying me again.*
> *No, I can't, I can't do this." He began. Retrospect is of course 20/20 and had I been able to go back to that moment there would have been a hundred things I would*

have done differently. Obviously overestimating the stun baton is a mistake I would not repeat. The other one was putting up with his bullshit. I should have just pounded him in the back of the head while he was down until he lay unconscious on the floor. I should have shut the big door when I had the chance but everything moved too quickly and I didn't want to take my eyes off him for one second.

He got back to his feet having removed the duct tape and when I pointed the gun at him again, he grabbed it. He gripped down hard, twice and I think I might have seen a gleam in him that indicated he felt the guns construction and realized it was not real but I can't be sure. I still held on for dear life, not willing to give him a blunt object to hit me back with.

Chapter 12: Nightmare on What Street?

After taking a few more blows, I quickly glanced at the garage door to make sure I was in the right position. When I could judge that I was close enough, I turned around having my back towards him and jerked forward in order to make sure he had a good hold on my jacket. Well in his grasp, I slipped out of the jacket and quickly dove downward and out. Throwing myself away from him and toward the garage door I landed on the garage floor and rolled out and onto the unpaved driveway. I was enveloped by the cool night air. Until that moment I hadn't realized how hot it had been in the garage.

Finally, outside of the garage door "Sheena" said she would leave open, I was elated. I made it back outside and escaped death! It was the greatest feeling in the world but it only lasted for about five seconds. When I got up and tried to run down the unpaved driveway, I couldn't. Like the nightmare, when I got up to run, my legs didn't work. I landed right beside my passenger door but I knew I wouldn't have time to unlock the door, and get in. At the time I figured it was because I was so tired from fighting. I tried to get back up but wasn't able to!

I began crawling and dragging my body across the gravel with my hands and nails, knowing my attacker would be after me at any second. I couldn't seem to get past the unpaved driveway. It was terrifying, knowing I was so close to escape! But, just as I had expected, as I was crawling and dragging my body across the gravel, I felt him grab my legs to drag me back into the garage. I tried to hold onto the loose gravel but I didn't have any strength to fight him anymore. I tried to grab a nice size rock from the driveway to use as a weapon, but he noticed and jerked my body until I dropped it. I thought, if I would have only been able to hold on to that rock I would have definitely tried to knock him out with it.

As the masked man continued dragging me back into whatever nightmare awaited me in that garage, I felt exhausted and crushed. Worse, I was out of ideas on how to get away. At that point I didn't know what I would do once back in the hot garage. I really thought I was out of luck and I would be doomed this time!

Twitchell's diary speaks of the event as if I'm an animal he is trying to trap for dinner:

Frank made a few feeble attempts to hit me and tried one impotent kick aimed at my groin that I easily deflected. I delivered a head butt to his face and he broke free again. I clutched onto his jacket but he shook himself loose of it and took off for the opening in the door.

He made it into the driveway and that's when I knew I was pooched. I followed him out, not caring anymore who might see me. He was fumbling on the ground. I grabbed him by the leg as if to drag him back into the garage caveman style but my energy was depleting and the human survival instinct is one of the most powerful forces on Earth.

Chapter 13: Stunned Batons

The courtroom was wrapped with attention when I said, "I kept letting him hit me and when I got to the door, he grabbed my jacket so I got out of my jacket and rolled out from under the garage. I remember thinking, 'Thank God!' It felt so good because it was so hot inside the garage."

With almost everyone's eyes on me, I continued, "I tried to run but my legs wouldn't work so I fell flat on my face. I don't know why my legs wouldn't work so I started crawling away." I took a deep breath and continued, "He then grabbed my legs and started dragging me back to the garage. I thought oh, I don't have a second plan."

Since then, I learned that I was probably feeling the effects of the stun baton.* My research tells me that the stun baton used high voltage and low amperage to temporarily disable me. The stun gun does not rely on pain for results, which is why I did not feel like it was doing anything to me at the time. The energy stored in the baton was dumped into my muscles causing them to do a great deal of work rapidly. This rapid work cycle instantly depleted my blood sugar by converting it to lactic acid. In short, I was unable to produce energy for my muscles, and my body was unable to function properly. The stun baton also interrupted the tiny neurological impulses that controlled and directed my voluntary muscle movement. When my neuromuscular system was overwhelmed and controlled by the stun baton I would lose my balance.

The actual stun baton used. The device is advertised as being capable of delivering "800,000 volts of stopping power" and can penetrate through a 1/2 inch of clothing."

Chapter 14: Real Life Horror Story

As my attacker was attempting to roll me back under the garage door, he had to let go of me for a second in order to get under the door himself. Noticing this, I took the opportunity to roll back out of the garage once again. It was my second chance to get away and I knew if I didn`t get some kind of strength to run, I would surely be dead this time. I got to my feet and gave it my best!

Somehow, I was able to get enough energy to stay up and run away this time, at least for a while. I thought that my adrenaline may have kicked in, or perhaps some angels were looking out for me. Happy to be out of his lair, I turned to the left down the alley. I noticed there was a wide-open space beside the house and a walking path lied directly beside the house's property line. The first thing that came to mind was to follow that path to the road in front of the house so I could flag down a passing car. But, as soon as I got to the relative safety of the walking path, I stumbled and fell onto it. Suddenly I was feeling very weak for some reason. I was forced to stand still, hunching over and trying to catch my breath, right smack in the middle of the walking path and the alley.

To my surprise, the walking path was inhabited. There was a couple walking their dog and a jogger in a red and white tracksuit. I didn't bother to stop the jogger since he passed by me quite quickly. I focused my attention on the couple, thinking I had finally found a way out of this! I assumed I wouldn't have to run any longer and they could help me out. When the couple got closer I was hunched over with sweat running down my bright red face. I was a mess from the struggle and all I could say was, "There's a guy after me…he's trying to mug me…please help me".

Shocked to come across such a scene on their stroll, the couple just stood there looking at me. I must have looked suspect, to say the least! At loss for words, they just watched me questioningly. As for the masked man, he took his time coming after me. Since he didn't give chase immediately, I assumed he needed to catch his breath or grab the handcuffs that I had thrown into a pile of other things.

When the man got to the walking path, he almost ran into the couple. Now there were four of us on that dusk path, and one of us was wearing a hockey mask and a hoodie! I pointed to him, looked at the couple and I said, "That's the guy!" The masked man seemed genuinely stunned to see other people around since he was disheveled from the fight and his mask was crooked and more to the left of his face. He was exactly the figure you meet on a dark path at night in your worst nightmares. Knowing he must have looked odd walking around like that, the masked man did something surprising. He turned to me and began to slightly pull up on his mask, as if he were going to take it off. Stopping before I could see his face, he merely said to me, "Come on Frank," as if he and I were friends and we were just fooling around. He tried to coax me back to the garage, walking towards it and calling me by this made up name. He started towards it, as if I would follow, but he stopped when he got to the unpaved driveway. He stood behind the fence, peering over like a nosey neighbour.

Still trying to catch my breath, the couple began to walk away. I assumed that they were freaked out by the whole "real life horror story" that was unfolding in front of them. Looking back towards my attacker, I noticed he had retreated into the garage. As soon as I saw that, I asked the couple if they were going to help me; I pleaded with them. Neither responded, but the male started to walk back towards me until his female partner called him back. I then asked them both, "Can you at least stand at the corner here and make sure I get back into my truck safely?" Again the male started coming back towards me but the female called him back, and he complied once again.

At this point I knew they weren't going to help me out so I angrily mumbled, "Never mind, I'll do it myself." I wasn't sure if they heard me or not, but at that point it didn't matter because it was clear to me they weren't going to help. Afraid for their own wellbeing, they walked off down the path looking behind them all the way home, all the while wondering what was really happening. Was I being mugged or was I in on it with the masked man in a plan to attack them? They had no way of knowing. Unsure whether anyone had been hurt or even whether or not they had been followed, as soon as they got home they called 9-1-1.

Chapter 15: Masks

Continuing where I left off, I testified, "I decided there's no way I'm not going to run this time so I put all my energy into running. It was probably more like a jog but at least I was moving!" Then I braced myself to talk about the couple. "I wanted to flag down a car but I saw three people ahead of me," I said, telling them that I saw a jogger and a couple.

At this point it was difficult to hold back my emotions again. Just shy of tears, I continued testifying about yelling to the couple, saying, "THERE'S A GUY ATTACKING ME, HE'S MUGGING ME, PLEASE HELP ME!" I told the courtroom, "I wasn't thinking straight at the time, which is why I needed somebody to help me." Sitting in the courtroom after all that time that's passed, it seemed insane that I forgot I had my cell phone on me. I was in such a state of shock that I didn't even think of the fact that I could have called 9-1-1 by myself.

SKConfessions was identical to my testimony:

He tried to grab at my mask and came quite close to pulling it off. I broke the grasp and he spun away into the alley and sure enough, a couple on an evening stroll saw me coming after him sporting a deer in the headlight look that can only be described as a total lack of comprehension. I stared back at them through my mask for half a moment and then headed back for the cover of my lair.

Chapter 16: Jacket Decision

Even though I wasn't thinking straight I was still smart enough to know that I suddenly had the advantage. The masked man had retreated to his garage and therefore he did not know if I was still with the couple. At this point I knew I had a few options to save myself. I could have followed the couple, but I assumed that I would just continue to scare them. I also thought of going onto the street in front of the house to try and stop a passing car. Then, I considered knocking on a neighbor's door to see if they could help me. In the end, I decided none of those alternatives were optimal.

As crazy as it sounds, I decided to go back to the garage and try to get back to my truck. This might have been a fatal decision, but I guessed the masked man still thought I was with the couple and I knew I would be a lot safer in a locked vehicle. I walked back to the garage as quietly as possible. From a distance I looked under the garage door. I could see the masked man's boots pacing back and forth beside my crumpled up black jacket. Since I wasn't thinking straight, for a second, I thought of trying to grab my jacket, but I quickly came to my senses. That jacket may have saved my life once...

Before I could change my mind or do something else stupid, I walked slowly down the unpaved driveway. Trying to make as little noise as possible, I took my truck keys out of my pocket and put them in the lock. I assumed the man could jump out at me at any moment so I unlocked my truck door very quietly. Once in, I knew that shutting the door would be the loudest part, but I knew that if he did come after me, the odds would be in my favour. I could start the truck and drive away and he would have to give chase and break through the window to get to me. I took a deep breath, shut the door, started the truck, put it into gear and quickly backed up into the alley. I paused briefly to see if he would come for me but when he didn't, I threw it in drive and raced ahead. I was going forward but from that moment on, I kept my eyes on the rearview mirror.

Chapter 17: Relief

I took a deep breath and continued to tell the court about the couple, "I thought maybe I should follow them but that would have probably freaked them out so I decided I was safest in my truck." I finished, looking at Avril and exhaling. It seemed meant to be for me to meet the couple since their testimony would prove without a shadow of a doubt that *SKConfessions* was completely true.

In *SKConfessions,* Twitchell wrote about his initial instincts after the incident:

I don't know why I played it as cool as I did. Maybe it was something Frank said during the skirmish about swearing not to tell anyone if I let him go. Maybe it was my own instincts about reading people and the fear in his eyes that told me deep down, he wouldn't report the incident, but I felt ok.

I still packed any gear up of my own and his stray jacket into a bag. Whatever I felt like keeping I cleaned prints off of and tossed the rest in a dumpster. As a final touch I sent one last warning email to Frank through the dating site telling him I had traced his IP address through his messages and that if he did report me, I would hunt him down where he lives when he least expects it and finish what I started. I threw in a line about having cased the garage, that it wasn't even mine and that I never use the same location twice. My last lie was to tell him he was lucky number eighteen on my spree.

I wasn't sure if I should believe it worked. I walked calmly out to my car, got in and drove away, across the entire city back to my home where my wife and child waited for me. During the entire trip I kept thinking surely this douche bag would call the police. Not that it mattered if he did. I covered my tracks well.

Chapter 18: The One Who Got Away

Deciding to follow my attacker's directions in reverse, I began the cross-city drive home. When I was a safe distance away, I checked the clock on my dashboard and saw that it was just past 8:00 PM. Although it felt longer, the whole ordeal had lasted less than an hour. I was afraid to think of what would be happening to me if I had been unable to get away. I shivered at the thought, and the first of many chills ran down my spine. I couldn't believe I had made it out alive!

It was starting to get darker and I although I tried to keep driving I began to feel terrible and I had to pull over. I was finally feeling the effects of the stun baton combined with and all of the blows to my head and body. I came down from my adrenaline high when I was by 98th Avenue and 75th Street. I took a right and pulled over in front of a Baptist church. Feeling like it was a safe omen, I got out of my truck to catch some air. My head and ribs were throbbing; I hurt everywhere and I felt really sick. I stood on the sidewalk facing away from the church trying to throw up, but nothing came out. It felt like I needed to expel something but the dry heaves were all my body could muster. It was as if I were trying to expel the Devil right there in front of that church!

I went back to my truck and found a bottle of water. I drank most of it in one gulp and then poured whatever was left on my face. I wanted to call somebody to come and help me but in that moment I felt that I didn't have anybody I *could* call. So, I just lay down in my truck for a while and rested, closing my eyes and leaning back, gingerly. Before I knew it, I woke up, not realizing I had fallen asleep! Somehow I passed out, but only for ten or fifteen minutes and I was still in a lot of pain.

Despite the short rest and crippling pain, I decided to try and get home. Driving up to the relative safety of my home, I was happy to see that none of my roommates were there. I had wanted to be alone for a while to process what had happened. I looked in the mirror and I was shocked to see how swollen the entire left side of my face was. I could barely move and I was ready to fall down, my muscles were so spent.

I grabbed some frozen vegetables and a towel and went to bed. A couple of hours later, I awoke with a towel of partially frozen vegetables on my face. I looked at a clock to see that it was still only 10:30 PM. I had been to hell and back, and even though the pain was severe, I forced myself to get up. I needed to log onto the online dating service to get some information. I figured I should get as much evidence as possible, in case I needed it for the police.

When I logged on to look for all of our messages, my first thought was that I was seeing things incorrectly. I blinked and looked again but it was the same - all of the incoming and outgoing messages we had sent one another had been deleted! I felt sicker by the moment! I quickly did a search for "Spiderwebzz"'s profile but it was gone too. Like it had never happened, there was no trace of this person! The only proof I had that the night had even happened, were the directions that she had given me. Fortunately I copied and pasted her pictures and the directions into a text document for printing. If I hadn't, even I would have had a hard time believing everything really happened.

I knew I should have called the police right away, but I decided to wait. I was in no shape to do anything that night! The only person I talked to about it was my ex-wife a few days later. I called her and told her about my ordeal, in great detail. In the end she urged me to go to police, and I agreed I would go the next day.

Chapter 19: The Aftermath

The courtroom quiet, Twitchell's head facing down, I continued talking about my escape and the pain I had been in. I said, "I wasn't thinking because I had my cell phone with me and I could have called the police but I didn't. I don't know why. When I got home I looked at myself in the mirror and saw how bruised I was." I told them that I iced my face to ease the immense swelling, pointing at my left temple.

I continued, saying, "I wanted to go online to get more info. But when I went back online all the information was deleted. All my messages with Spiderwebzz were gone, her profile, everything—gone."

"Did your attacker take anything or demand anything?"

"He said if you cooperate it will be a standard mugging and he'd let me go. I said take my watch, take my wallet, whatever."

"Describe the man," Prosecutor Ingles asked.

"He was taller than me, I'm five foot seven; he was a bigger build than me. I was probably one hundred and forty pounds then. I'm thirty-six now; I was thirty-three then. I forgot to mention I tried to pull his hockey mask off but it was on very tight. I thought he had red freckles or that the mask was rubbing against his face. I thought he was younger than me, I told the police I guessed he was twenty-two. I don't remember shoes but I thought he was wearing boots. No facial hair, his skin was white in colour," I said. When asked about the seeing the man in that garage, I said, "I've been trying to think of that for the past two and a half years but I didn't see where he came from. I don't know how I didn't see him."

Next, Prosecutor Ingles asked if I would be able to recognize the handcuffs if I saw a picture. I told her, "I work for security, so I'd recognize the handcuffs," and then she went ahead and showed me the exhibits. There were pictures of the handcuffs he was going to use on me. They were plain and black but very sturdy cuffs. I testified that they did appear to be the handcuffs that I had seen that day. Then I was shown pictures of the location, which I was able to correctly recognize. Avril spent a lot of time with me going over location photos and asking me to point out exactly where I was standing in proportion to the man and then the couple.

Twitchell wrote about how he would get away with my assault, despite feeling an impending doom:

You see in my day life I'm an independent film-maker and everything in that garage could be easily explained away as props for filming a psychological thriller. How I could be on one side of the city scrapping with a potential kill up until 7:20 PM and be home less than an hour later would have been a stretch at best.

Still, I couldn't shake the foreboding feeling. I kept thinking any moment I'd see flashing lights behind me asking me to pull over, despite my perfect adherence to posted speed limits and cautious observance of the safety belt law. Surely the arresting officer would wonder why I was so sweaty and why there was a bag with a hoody, a jacket, a prohibited stun weapon and a set of handcuffs in my trunk. But those lights never showed up in my rear view mirror.

I checked my voicemail messages and had two; very unusual this time of night. One from my wife wondering if I could be home by 8:30 so that she could pick up a package before 9:00 and one from my prop guy asking if he could borrow my airsoft pistol. Paranoia set in. My wife wouldn't care about picking up a package this late, she'd wait until tomorrow. Could the cops have gotten to her and convinced her to pretend to get me home quicker so they could arrest me?

But I had to stop and think clearly. This was all happening way too fast. There's no way that was possible, this wasn't a movie, this was real life. Even if the police were contacted, their response time to the location would be in the neighborhood of twenty minutes to two hours and there'd be no way for them to verify who rented the garage that quickly.

My fear subsided and I drove home. I practiced my entire behavior pattern should I come home to police cruisers parked along my front yard. I would rush the door in a panic and upon entering or being stopped by patrolmen I would appear utterly surprised and beg them to know if anything had happened to my precious wife and/or daughter. My genuine shock of their presence would start me on the innocent path in their eyes, and then my cover story of being at a therapy appointment would become my short term alibi until I could confess to the cops later that therapy was a cover story I gave my wife so I could have just one night a week to myself.

Between that and the total lack of hard evidence I'd be free regardless and yet still the nervousness set in.

It's pretty fucking hard to concentrate on anything when you live in constant expectation of the police arriving at your doorstep. It turns out my wife did need to pick up a package, a Pilates chair that she wanted me to assemble. The directions couldn't be any more complicated than the directions for making mac and cheese but I had a really hard time because the apprehension was always there.

Every time I heard a car drive by I'd feel compelled to look out the window. I heard a massive group of sirens get closer, and closer and closer. My heart leaped into my chest until I realized there was a house fire somewhere close to the area.

Seeing a police cruiser slowly and deliberately pull around my block was the worst part. But then I remembered our across the street neighbor had an itchy trigger finger for calling the cops when the rowdy teenagers next door partied too loudly and it subsided.

A day passed. I spent that day with my 8 month old daughter as my wife ran errands and kept appointments. Then the day turned to night and once again I was suspicious but nothing happened. That was the night I was totally convinced I had gotten off on this one pretty much scot free.

No patrol car would come to take me away bound in handcuffs to be brought up on assault charges, forever ending my serial killing career before it began and bringing down my marriage with it when my wife finds out what I really am.

That first time experience was the basis for my revised method of opperandi. Previously I wanted my victims alive and conscious after I had subdued them. I wanted to get information from them like their email and dating site passwords as well as the pin codes to their debit cards and credit cards. But this priority is now a distant second to making sure I don't get caught. I got lucky that first time and I wasn't going to assume that would ever happen again if anyone else got loose.

Chapter 20: Behind Me?

When the next day rolled around, I looked at my face in the mirror and was happy to see that the swelling had considerably gone down. Although my face was slightly bruised, it was not too obvious. Despite the intense pain in my ribs, I could function and move normally. Even though I had to work at the casino that night, I hoped nobody would notice my injuries.

Ashamed and embarrassed at what happened the night prior, I really didn't want to tell anybody about it. There were several reasons why I felt stupid about it. For one, I was using an online dating website in 2008, a time when online dating was still gaining social acceptability. Also, I had made some stupid errors that night. I shouldn't have kept the date a secret, making it impossible for someone to find me. In such a rush to meet someone, I had even disobeyed the number one rule in online dating: always meet in a public place. It's hard to explain just how humiliating it was to have been duped into believing I would be meeting a woman when it was really a man. Worse, the man wasn't in it for dating purposes at all, he wanted to kill me!

All I wanted to do was put the whole ordeal behind me and get on with my life! I thought that I could do just that by just trying to forget about the entire ordeal. The night after the attack, I was able to make my first public appearance at the casino where I worked without anyone noticing. I managed to move about gingerly and I avoided cringing in front of anyone when my ribs screamed out in pain. In retrospect, I wanted it to remain a secret so badly that I blocked out anything to the contrary. At the time, I didn't even hear a coworker and friend who said, "What happened to you?" I didn't find out that he said that until years later. So, thinking no one had noticed, I figured that my embarrassing secret was safe with me.

Two days after the attack, on October 5, my head still hurt and my ribs felt even worse than they had the day before. The pain was severe and it was everywhere. I tried to relax that day and I met my friend Rebecca for drinks that evening. She noticed my face immediately, which surprised me since I thought I had gotten away with it at work. When I told her what happened, she urged me to go to the police. I agreed with her at the time, but then changed my mind later.

In the following days, it was becoming harder to hide what had happened to me since the left side of my face was turning black and yellow. I was forced to tell all of my co-workers and they also pressed me to go tell my story to the police right away. I told them I would, and I meant it at the time. The following weekend, however, I drove down to Regina, Saskatchewan to celebrate Thanksgiving with my family. I had never been so thankful to see them in my life!

It seemed like the perfect time to spend some time with family. I was so happy to be alive and I was looking forward to seeing them all at once. Once again I had to tell my story, this time for my family. In the end, they were all very relieved that I was okay! Of course they counseled me to go to the police, and I agreed that I would go when I got back to Edmonton. For some reason, maybe it was fear of reprisal, but my family had also failed in convincing me to go to the police.

During the following weeks, I couldn't get my attack out of my head. I kept seeing my attacker everywhere! It was like I was hallucinating seeing a figment of him everywhere. He was there during the day and when I did manage to sleep, I had nightmares of the attack and of him coming for me. He was with me day and night, and every time I pictured the hockey mask, or his eyes, chills would run up and down my spine. At times, I truly believed he was following me so that he could finish the job that he had started. He could have been following me and plotting revenge for all I knew.

Everything changed again for me on the morning of November 2, 2008. I awoke to my phone ringing and ringing. I looked to see that my friend Andrew had been calling me over and over again. When I finally answered the phone, he told me to turn on my computer right away. He directed me to a news article from a Canadian news site. He said he had just seen something he thought might be related to my attack. Even though I couldn't imagine he would be right about it, part of me knew I had to get to my computer, and quickly.

Andrew said I would find an article about a filmmaker with a hockey mask. As I began reading, I realized that it had to be the same person. I couldn't believe it! The article said a man had ***killed*** somebody in a garage in the Millwoods area of Edmonton, Alberta. The alleged killer's name was Mark Twitchell. I was shocked at how similar it sounded to my experience, and it felt like I was outside of my body, reading an article about myself.

The article read:
Edmonton Police allege man made movie about murder
Updated: Sat Nov. 01 2008 18:37:28
Police allege a local film producer who has been charged with the first degree murder of an Edmonton man who went missing three weeks ago, carefully plotted the death and even made a movie about how he would do it.
Mark Andrew Twitchell,* 29, was arrested on Friday Oct. 31 at his parent's north Edmonton residence and has been charged for the first degree murder of 38-year-old Johnny Brian Altinger* who was last seen on Oct. 10.

*Mark Andrew Twitchell

*John Altinger

Altinger's body has not been found, but Detectives believe they have enough forensic evidence to lay first degree murder charges.

Friends of the 38-year-old victim say he met a girl online and agreed to meet with her, but Police say that was all part of the murder plot.

Twitchell had apparently made a movie about a man who is lured from an internet dating site and then murdered, just days before Altinger went missing.

"The movie was about luring a male from a dating internet site and basically killing the male in the garage and chopping up the body parts and getting rid of the body," said Detective Mark Anstey.

Homicide Detectives returned to the Twitchell residence on Saturday morning, along with the suspect, hoping he would lead them to Altinger's remains.

Police are also looking for another man who is believed to have been the original murder target.

The victim was able to break free and run into the lane while being chased by the male in a hockey mask, at *the same time a couple was walking by and saw the altercation," said Anstey.*

Police say they found a hockey mask* matching the description at Twitchell's home. It was the same hockey mask Twitchell used in his movie and Police allege it was likely the same one used in Altinger's death.

*The actual mask

Police do not believe Twitchell knew Altinger.

The bizarre details are being met with anger and sadness by Altinger's friends who reported the man missing on Oct. 16.

"Why is anybody's intention to kill somebody for nothing?" said friend Hans-Wilhelm Adam.

While that question may remain unanswered, Detectives are working to find Altinger and provide some closure for his loved ones.

-Sonia Sunger, ctvedmonton.ca

I was extremely shaken with what I read and saw! Words cannot describe how I felt in that moment.

I was glad I had been sitting down because I could feel my legs get weak. Seeing the mask gave me a chill down my spine. I was sure it was the same guy! Then, I viewed the news video that was linked to the article. It was titled, "CTV Edmonton: Erin Isfeld on the bizarre plot." News anchors Joel Gotlib and Erin Isfeld appeared and began talking about the incident. They were showing pictures of the victim, John Brian Altinger. Next they showed the garage where the murder took place, the garage where I had just been. Then they showed the suspected killer's picture along with the hockey mask the murderer wore - the same mask my attacker wore! It was all very surreal. I felt like I was watching someone else's story play out on TV. The video showed Detective Anstey explaining the story, saying that they were still looking for another potential victim... Me! They were looking for me. The Detective went on to say that they needed to speak to the man that was the original target but got away. Erin Isfeld finished by saying,

Homicide Detectives want to stress that the other victim that they are looking for in this case is not in trouble but could help in the Altinger investigation. The man is:

-5'10", 180–190 lbs.

-Well-dressed, wearing a gold shirt.

-May be dark-skinned or tanned complexion.

-Hair in a tight perm with gel in it.

-Has a welt over his left eye.

-His name may be Francis, Hank, or Fred.

-May be driving a black Ford Ranger.

If you have any information on this individual please call the Police or Crimestoppers at 1-800-222-TIPS.

Still on the phone with Andrew, I silently contemplated my next move. He asked me if it was the same guy I had the run in with. "Yes, I'm positive." After seeing the video footage, I couldn't deny it. I wouldn't forget that part of his face that he let me see and I couldn't ever forget those eyes that were haunting my dreams. It was him alright. I felt like I couldn't move, like I was stuck in cement from head to toe. I had to will myself to move.

I was astonished that the police knew about me and needed to talk to me. The media knew about me! Andrew fervently insisted I talk to the police now since they were actually looking for me. *Now,* it would be against the law if I didn't come forward. I told him I would definitely go and talk to the police that very afternoon, and for the very first time, I actually meant it.

I'll admit I was extremely nervous. After weeks went by, I became more and more certain that I wasn't going to the police. I just wanted to go on with my life and put everything behind me. That was until the story became much bigger than me. Now, a man had been killed by the psycho who attacked me! Now the *only* thing to do was to tell the police my story.

Before leaving for the station I reviewed the video footage over and over. I still had a hard time believing I had made it on the news. I realized that *I* should be the one that was killed and *my* body should have been hacked up into pieces. It was incredibly hard to comprehend! Worse, I started to think that if only I would have gone to the police, John Brian Altinger might be alive and well right now. If I had just gone like I said I would, nobody would have been killed and dismembered. Guilt overwhelmed me.

Chapter 21: Cross Examination

In court when I was testifying, "A friend of mine called me on November second because I had told my story to him; he was a colleague. And he told me that he had checked out an article from CTV and I went online and saw the photo of the mask. They said they were looking for a first victim, so I decided to go forward. They came to my house and took the hard drive and replaced it with another." And that was the only time Twitchell looked up at me, for whatever reason.

At 11:30 AM, the defense attorney, Charles Davison began his cross-examination. He began by saying, "You were lying in the garage with the tape over your eyes and hands behind your back this is when you heard the jingles? You said those looked like the handcuffs that day?" For some reason, Twitchell put his head up at this moment and stared at me throughout the whole cross examination and I stared back at him as often as I could to let him know that I was no longer scared of him. "You have to admit that you can't really identify it definitively?" Davidson asked.

"Unfortunately not, there weren't any markings on it," I replied.

"You told us you were mainly intent on going to the pedestrian door? And you didn't see anything else in the garage at that time?" Davidson asked.

"I don't remember exactly, I was fighting for my life at this point. I don't remember what I saw. I couldn't tell you any details," I had to admit.
"Fair enough, but the general description was that it was fairly empty?"

"It seemed that way, yes." And my testimony was done. I sighed relief and was able to sit down and watch as the couple testified.

Twitchell's diary showed that afterwards, he wanted to be sure he got it right next time:

So I had to revise my apprehension system in order for it to go more smoothly. I decided to ramp up the savagery of my attack, leaving no margin for error in rendering a target unconscious within the first ten seconds. I dropped the stun baton for the favor of two 24 inch lengths of galvanized steel piping. I was confident that swinging for the fences to the back of the head would do the trick. I would go on a shopping trip the next day to make it happen.

Chapter 22: Coming Forward

At 1:30 pm on the afternoon of November 2, I drove to the North Division Police Station on Fiftieth Street. By chance, the station I needed to go to was the station closest to my house. Just three days earlier, my attacker, my attempted murderer, and John's killer had been arrested and charged with first-degree murder. It seemed to be no coincidence that October 31 was Mark Twitchell's favourite day of the year. It turned out my attacker had planned to wear a homemade Ironman costume for the holiday almost as intricate as the movie version. Every year Twitchell loved to create costumes which in 2007 he won first place at two Edmonton Halloween celebrations for a Bumblebee Transformer costume. That year he had won a Harley Davidson motorcycle and thousands of dollars. I was truly happy he didn't get the chance to enjoy Halloween one last time. In previous years it was parties and prize money and this year, it was bending over naked and coughing. I couldn't help but smile at the thought.

I was very nervous to talk to the Edmonton Police Department after all that time. When I first walked into the station, there were two other people. A woman was in line ahead of me and a man was already being helped. Before long, another Officer came in and helped the woman while I waited. When the woman was finished I was dismayed to see that the man was still talking to an Officer. I really didn't want to tell my story in front of a lot of people! I also knew that I had no choice. It wasn't like I could back away now! Fortunately, just as I began to talk to the Officer, the man left. I breathed a sigh of relief, happy that I would only have to tell my story to one person, not a roomful.

I took a deep breath and then I quietly said, "Do you know about the story in the paper about that filmmaker that killed that guy in that garage?"

"Yes."

"Uumm…well the guy that survived the first attack…That was me…I believe you guys are looking for me." I felt like I had just vomited all over his desk. The officer's eyes widened and his jaw dropped. He hesitated and then said, "Wait here," and then he quickly headed to the back. Being the lone person at the front desk calmed me down, but only a little. When the officer finally came back, he sat down at a desk and made a phone call. I stood for about a minute watching him talk to the person, and then he came over to me and said, "Pick up the phone over there in back of you on the wall and call this extension." When I did as he asked, Detective Mark Anstey, lead investigator, picked up the phone. I remembered seeing him on the news video talking about the case, and I was surprised to be talking to him a few hours later.

Detective Anstey began by telling me that they had been looking for me for a long time. He said they were very happy that I came in. After those pleasantries, he asked me to tell him a little about what happened and how I got away. I had the feeling he was testing me a bit to see if I was the right guy. I imagine they have a lot of wackos coming forward at times like this. When he heard what I had to say, he must have known immediately I was the guy. Telling my story, I may as well have been reading from Twitchell's diary, *SKConfessions.*

Detective Anstey asked for my name, address and the phone number he could reach me at. Then he asked me for my height, weight and a description of the clothes I was wearing that day. I said, "I'm Caucasian, approximately five feet, seven inches and one hundred forty pounds with short dark hair. That night I was wearing a black buttoned up short sleeve shirt and jeans." I said, remembering the description.

"Did we get anything right?" He then asked me laughingly.

I could have walked around unnoticed given how bad the description of me had been. No one would have guessed it was me that every media outlet was talking about. The only description they had to go by was the one given to them by the couple, who didn't see me very well. This was the actual information given out from the Edmonton Journal:

A different man was allegedly lured to the same garage on Oct. 3, and was attacked by a man wearing a hockey mask.

"The victim was able to break free and run into the lane while being chased by the male in the hockey mask," Edmonton homicide Det. Mark Anstey said.

A couple was walking by and saw the altercation. They described the man attacked, "He may drive a black Ford Ranger," Anstey said.

He is five-foot-10, approximately 180 to 190 pounds. He was well dressed that evening, wearing a gold shirt. He may possibly be tanned or dark skinned. His hair was in a tight perm with gel in it. He had welts over his left eye. And his name may possibly be Francis, Hank or Fred.

This man is not in trouble. He is a victim of an attack similar to what happened to Altinger, and Officers just want to speak with him.

-CanWest MediaWorks Publications Inc. - Published Monday, November 1, 2008

I responded laughingly that the only thing they got right was that I drove a black Ford Ranger. Next he asked me to describe the woman that I was talking to online. I said, "her name was 'Sheena,' she was five foot six, she had blonde hair and she was fairly good looking."

"That's odd! Mr. Altinger's woman was a redhead and her name was Jen," Anstey said.

The Detective then asked who the first person I had told the story of my attack to, so they could confirm my story. I told them that I believed it was my ex-wife, Pamela. He then asked her for her phone number which I gladly gave to him.

Lastly he asked if I could come to the main downtown station the next day, November 3, 2008. Of course, I agreed and an interview was scheduled for 2:00 PM. It would be exactly one month since the attack. I was told to park at the police lot and to call him directly when I arrived so he could meet me in the lobby. He gave me his personal cell phone number and his email address and told me to bring anything I thought might help them out with the case. "I have the directions she gave me and the three pictures of the woman," I said. The Detective seemed happy with this new information. I felt a weight starting to lift.

When I hung up the phone, I informed the on duty Officer about my meeting the next day, and he seemed happy to hear it. I walked out of the police station and drove home with my mind on anything but the road; I got home without remembering a single turn or stoplight. I was nervous about the next day, unsure whether I was more relieved than scared. I had never been interviewed by a homicide detective before. My only frame of reference came from the movies and TV, which was what my life was beginning to feel like. It was as if I had the feeling of watching myself from the outside.

As if to prove the point, I found an article that night that showed how fast news travelled. Apparently, my movements were being tracked by journalists, and it was not a comfortable feeling. My life was feeling more like an out of body experience by the second. It seemed like everyone in the world knew what was happening in my life, right after it happened to me! The article reported that police had found the second victim, and they reported about our plans for an interview the next day:

Meanwhile, Police say another man was lured to the same garage on Oct. 3, also intending to meet with a woman he had met online. This second man was allegedly attacked by a man wearing a hockey mask, but was able to escape.

Two neighbours said they spotted a man running away from the garage that night, fleeing another man who was wearing a black and gold hockey mask.

Police seized a black and gold mask from Twitchell's residence over the weekend.

Police said they had located this second man following Twitchell's arrest, but have not yet had the chance to interview him.

-Amanda Ferguson, ctvedmonton.ca - Published Monday, November 3, 2008

Chapter 23: The Detective Clark Interview

As planned, I drove down to the Downtown Division Police Station for a 2:00 PM interview on November 3, 2008. All morning I had been nervously waiting, jittery from a lack of sleep. When I finally got to the station, I noticed a couple of news reporters had camped out by the front doors. I had a weary feeling they might ambush me with questions, but then I remembered that the media's description of me was way off! Indeed, I was able to walk right past all of them without a second glance. Part of me was surprised that none of them suspected *I* was the one they were desperately wanted to talk with. I was the guy they would soon be calling, "the one who got away."

Although he told me to call him directly, I wasn't yet comfortable calling a homicide detective's cell phone. Instead, I walked directly to the front desk and asked the officer behind the glass partition to let Detective Anstey know I was there. He asked my name and then told me to "have a seat and the Detective would be right down." I saw that there were many seats available, allowing me to select a chair right in front of the main doors so Detective Anstey would see me as soon as he got there. Waiting nervously, I tried to make myself comfortable in such an uncomfortable setting. Knowing that I was about to have an interview with a homicide detective, the hard seats felt more awkward than they really were.

After a couple of minutes, Detective Anstey, lead Detective on the Twitchell case, walked through the big security doors and straight to me. Without speaking, we took the elevators to the third floor. I was intensely aware of everything, as if watching a gripping movie that *I* had the lead role in. Time seemed to slow down. When the elevator doors opened, I had no idea where the detective was taking me, but I followed him anyway. We went deeper and deeper into the labyrinth of hallways. We finally went through some doors with an unpretentious sign overhead reading, "HOMICIDE DIVISION." Seeing it in print, the movie I was imagining felt a bit more "real." The Detective brought me to a place where they had many small interview rooms, just like the ones on TV and in the movies. He asked me to enter Room One, and I complied. The first thing I noticed was a pink love seat on the left. There was also a single chair in the far right corner, which I assumed would be for the interrogator. I didn't know it at the time, but I had just entered what detectives called a "soft" room. Since I was a witness, not a suspect, I had the advantage of having a more comfortable environment. Despite this, just being there made me feel like I might be guilty of something, even though I knew I wasn't. Detective Anstey told me that I should sit on the loveseat and then he told me that he wouldn't be the one to take my statement. He said that a Detective named Bill Clark would be interviewing me. Unbeknownst to me at the time, Clark was the department's "star" interrogator. Detective Anstey left the room.

Sitting alone and waiting felt surreal. The room was extremely tiny, the pink loveseat covering a good portion of the wall. The small room also had a coffee table with a lamp, a box of Kleenex, and a Bible, so you could swear you had just told the truth. I wondered how many murderers had sat where I was sitting now, waiting nervously for the detective to walk through that door. Looking around, I noticed a white object at the top of ceiling and wondered if I were being watched and or listened to. I'm glad I didn't know at the time, but detectives were in fact watching and listening in.

It felt like the wait was forever. Unbeknownst to me, the detectives sat in another room making mental and verbal observations about my body language. They would have seen that I was still very nervous, slightly paranoid and worried about what the detective might ask me. I had no idea what to expect, feeling guiltier the longer I waited. When Detective Clark finally opened the door and came in, he sat down in the chair and said,
Okay. What I want you to do Gilles is just basically walk me through everything and what I'll do is I'll just let you ramble on. I might write a few things down, I might not. I want you to start right at the beginning from any first contact how it developed. All that type of stuff and then I'll probably have some questions for you afterwards. Just take your time. We got as long as it takes. There's no rush here so start right at the beginning.
And just like that, the interview had begun!

Even though it was traumatic, I started recounting my story. He needed to know every miniscule detail, so it felt like I was reliving it all over again. I was getting chills down my back recalling what happened. Little did I know he was also getting chills listening to me tell him the story he had read in an allegedly fictional "script" that was found in the deleted files of Twitchell's laptop. Named "SKConfessions," it was a play-by-play account of an attempted murder and a murder. According to Twitchell, "SK" stood for Stephen King, not serial killer, but the entire courtroom was about to realize how accurate the diary was. Our accounts match almost exactly where he is talking about the part I played in his "script." The document includes the author's extensive planning, and successful second attempt at murdering men lured to his garage using fake online dating profiles. It also describes the process of dismembering the victim's body and his numerous attempts to dispose of the remains.

Once I was finished, Detective Clark said, "Okay. That's quite the story. It's amazing it's... I guess you realize how lucky you were."

"I thought I was... after this all happened I realize how lucky I was. But not until now... it's so much bigger," I stammered.

"Yeah. And you know what [and] I appreciate it's hard for you to relive it."

"Yeah." I said, "I get shivers down my back!"

"I can see it, but you know what I appreciate your honesty and that's all I'm here for, I'm not here to judge you." Detective Clark reassured me. He said, "I'm just here to get the information we need to put this guy away for a long time. And we really appreciate you coming forward, because it's so important to this investigation."

"I just didn't know what he would have done to me," I said.

"It's just a bizarre situation. The whole thing, you know?" Detective Clark said, reassuringly. He wasn't judging me, but I was judging myself for not coming forward. I was feeling extremely guilty that a man had died and I might have been able to do something to stop it.

Detective Clark then told me he had to take me through it again. He said he had to clarify a few things, like the day it all happened. I told him that it was October 3 and showed him my proof: a copy of the directions and a map printed from Google showing how to get to the garage from my house. I also showed him the actual email from "Sheena" giving me the directions to the garage, and the three pictures of the blonde female that I thought I was talking to. Detective Clark asked me to sign my name on each page and said he would have to keep them. Then, he asked me a lot of questions about Plenty of Fish, where I met "Sheena." He asked me about the woman's online name, "Spiderwebzz," and said he wanted to make sure he spelled it correctly. He wondered how long I had been using the site and what email addresses I used on it. I supplied the email addresses and estimated that I had been on the site since May 2008. He asked me what name I went by while talking to Sheena and I told him I used the name "dr_x." When he asked if I used my real name at all, and I felt badly that I couldn't remember since I sometimes use the fake name of Brian until I get to know the person better. I also made sure to tell him, "It's not the site's fault." I said, "the site is a very good place to meet people, it's just there are some sick people out there."

"Yeah, obviously." Detective Clark said. Another shiver ran down my spine thinking of Twitchell. Next, Detective Clark asked me if I had a problem with his tech guys looking at my computer. He told me that he wasn't concerned about anything else on the computer except for what they needed for the case. He also assured me his tech guys would be able to find the deleted messages between "Sheena" and myself. He let me know they would probably take a copy of my hard drive and that it would take a couple of days to do that. I responded that I would do anything to help out with the investigation and I wasn't worried about anything they may find on my computer. I mentioned it would be listed on the sent and received messages if they were able to retrieve them. I asked if they could get a hold of Plenty of Fish and get them to give them that information. He responded that they were going to, but they would have to do it through a search warrant and that took months to complete. By getting it off my computer, everything would happen a lot faster and I was happy to help. Then the Detective asked if Sheena had been forward with me and then he moved on to the directions she gave me, asking if I had any difficulty finding the garage. I explained that I had no trouble at all finding the garage with the yellow doors and the right garage door that was part way open with an unpaved driveway. Also, it was hard to miss the crappy sofas and other garbage.

The most difficult part of the interview was when Detective Clark even asked me to reenact the situation. He asked me to stand up and show him how high the garage door was open. When I got up, I showed him that it was probably about waist high and that I didn't need to crawl in. I demonstrated how I was able to squat down slightly to enter the garage. I also acted out the positions I was in during the struggle, showing him exactly what took place. At times, he would look down so he could write things down on his clipboard. He asked me to describe what I saw when I first got into the garage. I told him that at first, all I could remember was that it was very dark. Once my eyes adjusted, I saw a window to the right on the west end wall and a pedestrian door to the left end corner on the south wall. The next thing he asked if there was anything ever exchanged in emails about why I couldn't go to the front or why an address wasn't given. I told him about how she had told me that I couldn't park in the front and that her basement apartment was at the back of the house. I told him that I asked her again and again for an actual address or phone number, but she either avoided the question or said it was for security reasons.

Chapter 24: Meeting the Couple

On April 1, after I was done testifying, the couple was up next. I felt extremely relieved to be finished. I was as relaxed as I could be at a murder trial while I watched the couple testify about that night we met in the alleyway. It was difficult to hear them going through their story. When they were both finished testifying, I noticed that the couple left the courtroom and headed to the waiting room. I didn't think much of it and continued to watch the trial. While I watched the prosecution's courtroom process, I was happy to see their air-tight case unfold. This was the first time I had been able to watch any of the trial, and now that I was finished testifying, I could watch as much or as little as I wanted.

Shortly after the couple left the courtroom, Detective Bill Clark approached me. He tapped me on the shoulder and whispered for me to come with him. As I was exiting the courtroom I noticed that many of the reporters thought I was leaving, so they began following us out. I was really beginning to understand how important I was to the case and to the media. When we got out of the courtroom, just outside the waiting room doors, Detective Clark told me what was going on. The couple had to leave soon and they wanted to make sure they met with me. I confidently walked into the waiting room, looked up at the couple, gave them a big smile and introduced myself. I shook Trevor's hand and he introduced himself to me. When I turned to face Marisa, she gave me a great big hug, which surprised me, but made me happy. They both said they were genuinely sorry that they didn't help me that night. Talking with them added to my sense of closure. Not only was my testimony over and done with, I had found a new kinship with Trevor and Marisa. It was as if we had a wake right there outside the courtroom. The trial booming ahead without us, I forgave them, allowing them to put some of their guilt to death.

Once we were ready to leave the waiting room, Detective Clark suggested that because of the media frenzy, I should take the front entrance and that Trevor and Marisa take the back entrance of the courthouse. We all left and parted ways. As soon as I got out, I saw several reporters standing around. I immediately stopped in my tracks and Detective Clark approached me and suggested that I should go talk to them because if I didn't, they would continuously follow me all the way out of the courthouse. I agreed and walked up to the media crowd and told them that it was a long and emotional day for me; I would not be making any comments today but would answer their questions on another day. They all seemed to understand and agreed not to ask any questions. David Ewasuk from CTV News looked at me and told me that I gave an incredible testimony and that I was a very good storyteller. I thanked him and everybody else agreed. They then all started handing out their business cards to me and I graciously accepted them. I even got an envelope handed to me from Ronna Syed, a reporter for the *Fifth Estate*, a Canadian investigative program. I found it odd that she was handing me an envelope. Inside there were letters containing information on the television program that they wanted me to interview for about the harmful effects of online dating. They later decided to scrap that and filmed more on the whole Twitchell story.

I then went back to grab Detective Clark and the women who worked in Victims Services. We all went to the elevator and took it down to the main floor. From there, we went out the front exit of the building. That's when I saw dozens of camera men and reporters waiting for me. They started to film me talking to the two ladies. They wanted to chat with me a little outside before leaving, but to be frank, I don't even remember what they were saying. All I could concentrate on was how I was going to get through this crowd. I finally thanked the women for coming and left with Detective Clark. We went down the concrete stairs and with his help I got through the crowd but they were in my face with the cameras. I was so nervous. I didn't know how I should walk and smile and I prayed that I didn't fall down. A few reporters were apparently absent when I addressed the reporters earlier, so they were asking me questions. I just kept telling them that I wasn't going to comment at this time. We finally got to the street crossing and it felt like forever for the cross walk sign to change. Eventually, we crossed the street and headed back to the police station. Reporters continued to follow us. We continued to walk down the sidewalk and they finally backed off once we arrived at the police station. I entered the station front doors and Detective Clark opened the security doors and continued to the all-too-familiar Homicide Unit on the fourth floor. From there we went back to Detective Clark's office so he could drop off his things and then told me that he wanted me to meet somebody. He took me over to Detective Brad Mandrusiak's office.

Detective Clark introduced me to Detective Mandrusiak but I could tell he knew all about me already. The gentlemen shook my hand, offered me a beverage and Detective Clark brought me a Coke. I started to drink my pop and Detective Mandrusiak commended me on coming forward to tell my story. Unfortunately he wasn't able to see my testimony at the courthouse since he was scheduled to testify after me. We talked more about the trial and Mark Twitchell. Detective Mandrusiak then asked me if I would be willing to go through this all again if there was another trial for my attempted murder charge. I told him that I would definitely do it all again even if just to help to maybe put him away for longer. It was a nice change of pace being at the police station as if I was chatting with friends rather than being interviewed or tested for DNA evidence. Various other people approached me in the office just wanting to offer their respect, which I found surprising since I felt myself to be a pretty average guy. I continued in these conversations for a while until we decided to leave.

I followed Detective Clark and we exited the police station into the police parking lot and got into Detective Clark's personal vehicle, a black Pontiac. We left the parking lot and began to head home. That's when I started to get to know Bill on a more personal level. He told me about his family and that he had four sons. The Detective then took me to lunch, which I thought it was very nice of him to offer, even though my nerves were fried from my testimony and I wasn't sure I could eat anything. We drove to the North Town Centre Mall. Detective Clark paid for lunch. I could tell he genuinely wanted to treat me to a meal. We got our food and sat down and continued to chat about the trial. We chatted some more about what a ridiculous story Twitchell gave about buying a car for forty dollars and that also they had tracked down the female that I thought I was going to meet that day. Her name was obviously not Sheena and she lived in Brazil. Apparently he went on the Plenty of Fish website and searched for Brazilian women and found a girl that he thought would be attractive and saved her images from her profile onto his computer. Using those pictures, he then created a new profile here in Edmonton with the name of Spiderwebzz. It appears that the police contacted her and she had no clue about any of this. She was not impressed that her pictures were being used in this way. That information floored me. I was shocked that Twitchell had used another woman's identity in that way.

Chapter 25: Media Frenzy

When I finally got home from testifying, I felt like a different person. As if I had exercised a demon, I was lighter, happier even. But when I turned on the TV, the first thing I saw was an artist's rendering of myself from court.* All of the local news channels had this picture, my picture! It seemed like every time I changed the channel, the news just happened to be showing it. I felt like I was watching a movie about myself. Words can hardly describe how it felt.

The actual drawing that aired on CTV.

I had watched these newscasters on TV report the news to me for years and now they were telling me all about myself. Hearing my story told back to me, it felt as if it were someone else's story. It was hard to believe I had lived it, even though it haunted me day and night. It felt like I was in a room full of people who were talking about me, but not talking to me. I had just got home from court and they already knew everything. I was getting a lesson in just how fast news travels these days!

The day after I testified, April 2, 2011, I was stopped at a light when I noticed a newspaper box with a huge picture of me on it. The cover of the Edmonton Sun had a photograph, not an artist's drawing. In massive print next to my face, it read, "HE CHEATED DEATH."* I couldn't believe I was on the front page of the newspaper! Thinking that I had better read the story, I went to buy the local papers at 7/11. I quickly grabbed two papers, the Edmonton Sun and the Edmonton Journal. My picture didn't make the front page of the Journal, so I tried to make it less awkward by placing it on top and keeping the papers together when I went to the cashier. I breathed a sigh of relief when my plan worked and the clerk was none the wiser. Before I could leave the store, however, another man entered the store and grabbed the Sun. It had my picture on the cover and as he walked past me to the counter he gave it and me a double take. The man was unable to hide his jaw dropping reaction, but he never said anything. More and more, it felt as if I was a fly on the wall, looking in on my own life!

The Edmonton Sun, April 2, 2011

Not all of the headlines were as gratuitous as the Sun's. Some titles were less dramatic and more descriptive, like "Date turned into fight for life, man tells murder trial," "Alleged victim recounts fight for his life," and "Man tells Twitchell jury of attack in garage." After that, every media outlet started calling me "the one who got away." I didn't know how to feel about it. I found it hard to separate the fight for my life from John being murdered. How could I feel good about surviving when entire families had been shattered? It was a hard line to walk; feeling elated I was alive but devastated that John was not.

On April 3, 2011, I found a message waiting for me on Facebook from Marisa. Marisa then gave me the greatest gift she could have. She told me she had written me a letter expressing her remorse. I will always treasure the letter she wrote:

Hello my friend, just wanted to talk to you to tell you I am very sorry about the events that transpired on October 3. I know you just met us, but you should know that Trevor is a wonderful man, and on that night he really did want to help you, but his love for me is what stopped him. He loves me more than any love I've ever seen in movies or real life, and all he wants is for me to be safe and happy. I was so scared that night as soon as I saw that mask it was like every nightmare I've ever had come back to me and I thought "oh my god, this is actually it, the end, " I thought that the 2 of you were setting us up to rob (and it was the ONE time I went walking without taking anything with me but a house key) and that we were going to die. (I know you know that feeling). If I hadn't been there Trevor would have carried you to the hospital I'm sure, but his biggest worry was me. It was my fault we ran away. I was so scared and so panicked and I just wanted to get out of there. Trevor was stuck between thinking you were going to rob us and that you actually DID need our help. It was probably the biggest shock of both of our lives. When we ran home (we weren't very fit at the time so it took longer than it should have), we called my mom and then the Police. Once the Police came (there was a LOT of them, at least 5 and they had 2 dogs), Trevor took them back to the spot where the incident happened. When nothing came of it and no one came forward to the Police we were so positive that it had been a set up for us to be robbed, but still Trevor worried about you. He hated himself for leaving and probably woulda tackled that fucker had I not been there. He thought about you every day and wondered. Then all this stuff started coming out and it was so overwhelming. Trevor started thinking that his co-workers were the masked man. Anyways, that wasn't the point, but please know that Trevor so desperately wanted to help you, but his love for me and his need to make sure I was safe won out. He wouldn't abandon the love of his life when there was a chance that I could be hurt. He beats himself up daily now, thinking that he could've done more to help you and to save Johnny. I try to tell him he did all he could but it never helps. I hate Mark Twitchell with everything in my body for messing with us but hopefully he gets exactly what he deserves. And I hope you are ok too. If someone asked me today to name my "hero" I'd have to say it's a toss-up between you and Trevor, you fought so hard for your life when you had to, and I know Trevor would die for me if it ever came to that. I thought after facing the bastard I'd feel better but he didn't even look at me. Assface. I hope he rots in hell and that someday I will get a full night's sleep...lol.

For me, both the meeting and the letter were two giant steps towards closure. I hope they continue to forgive themselves for not helping me that night. I believe that John would probably want all of us to forgive ourselves. At least that is the impression I get from what I've learned about who he was as a person. Maybe he would be happy to know that I am working towards forgiving myself for not coming forward immediately, step by step.

For the following week, I tried my best to get my life back on track. I needed to focus on work and taking care of my two-year-old son, the product of a failed but fruitful relationship with his mother. I struggled to avoid hearing about the case and I faltered. Prior to my testimony, I kept abreast of the case, using a scrapbook for newspaper articles. I was grateful to learn that Twitchell's first defense attorney, David Cunningham, lost his argument for Twitchell to be released into the custody of his parents with a cash bail of $10,000. The argument for that must have been laughable to say the least. The details of the decision to deny bail were not released because of a publication ban however, in general, a judge may deny bail under Canadian law for two reasons, if:

1. a judge believes an accused person is a flight risk or if they feel the public needs to be protected from the accused

2. a judge decides it is necessary to maintain the public's confidence in the justice system

-Canadian Criminal Procedure and Practice/Release and Attendance/Judicial Interim Release

Chapter 26: The Final Verdict

After the fact, I learned all of the details I missed about the case, before and after I entered the courtroom and gave my testimony. I find it interesting that one of the few times Twitchell showed any real emotion, unsurprisingly, was when it came to his freedom. When Crown Prosecutor Avril Inglis countered the defense's reasoning for limiting his freedom, he began raising his eyebrows and shaking his head. Everyone already knew he was a psychopath, only concerned with his own needs, but he proved the point for us in that moment. When the judge finally announced that she was denying bail, Twitchell really showed how upset he was by storming out of the courtroom and out the prisoner's door as fast as he could. As someone who is in tune with other people's feelings and emotions, I found it incredibly difficult to be around Twitchell. I doubt I was the only one who found his emotionlessness, or emotional inappropriateness, hard to understand. When in his presence, the tiny hairs on the back of my neck rose and just the thought of him caused a chill to go down my spine.

It wasn't until September 4, 2009, that we had the first big victory in the court case when the Crown won their application for a direct indictment against Twitchell. This meant a preliminary hearing wouldn't be necessary, making everything move a lot faster. As things kept falling into place in the case against my attacker, it did little to ease my mind. I was saddened to learn that Twitchell chose to plead not guilty to murder and guilty to a much lesser charge of "improperly interfering with a dead body." Some of the proof used against him included 222 blood impact stains on the inside of the garage door, as logged into evidence by a Detective Chafe.

In another case of art imitating life, Detective Chafe testified right after being in Miami where he was teaching others about his specialty, blood spatter analysis. Having testified in over 40 criminal cases, his part in the Twitchell case was critical as well as ironic. Twitchell's idol, "Dexter," lived and worked in Miami as a blood spatter analyst in Jeff Lyndsay's dark series of novels. Detective Chafe testified that multiple impacts were needed to cause that much blood to spray out onto the bay door. In a twist of fate, Chafe's testimony would help to close the coffin on Twitchell's attempt to claim that it was self-defense. It was a heinous act, anyway you looked at it and every glaring detail reminded me of what could have happened to me. It could have been my blood on and under that garage door.

While on the stand, Twitchell told the jury that it was all a misunderstanding and he never meant to hurt John or me. He claimed that John attacked *him* when he didn't understand the "big joke," leaving him with no choice but to defend himself. It was a last-ditch effort to save Twitchell at best and a smart move by his lawyer at worst. If you believe *SKConfessions* to be accurate, as I do, then you will know that John was hit over the head repeatedly as soon as he entered that garage. Seven days after I escaped, John was bludgeoned with a lead pipe that Twitchell purchased just for that occasion. It was his Plan B, after the stun baton failed to work on me. To kill John, Twitchell wrote about stabbing him in the chest, and watching him bleed out on his garage floor. Twitchell chopped his body into pieces and burned them in the steel drum he claimed was for the film shoot.* Twitchell couldn't get the body parts burning long enough to do much damage, let alone incinerate them. He didn't know he needed to add oil to keep the body burning, and he was forced to come up with a plan C when the smoke began to rise above the house and unrelated sirens scared him into stopping. At that point, he chopped up the body into smaller pieces, this time taking more time to really examine the body parts. After putting everything back into black garbage bags, he drove around like that for a while, feeling smug when the police drove by.

**Twitchell's car with the drum he used.*

The first version of *SKConfessions* stopped right before the author got to the part about dumping the body. During the investigation, the police went back to Twitchell's computer and managed to find a newer copy of the document and this one had an ending. Twitchell said he dropped the body parts in a sewer, they learned, leading to a several-hour manhunt. They squirreled cameras down blocks worth of sewers, but they couldn't find John anywhere. The document didn't say which sewer and detectives tried to get the information out of Twitchell, but he wouldn't talk.

In an inexplicable move, almost two years later, on another Friday and another third of the month, on June 3, 2010, Twitchell and his new lawyer, Charles Davidson, called a meeting with Detectives in the Edmonton Remand Center. The rules were simple: no media, no questions, and no Detective Bill Clark. The detective that I had grown to know and admire had become Twitchell's chosen nemesis. It made sense because Clark had been the one to first confront Twitchell with the statement, "There is absolutely no doubt in my mind that you are involved with the disappearance of John Altinger!" So, two detectives visited Twitchell and his lawyer without the presence of Clark. They were handed a piece of paper and that was the end of the meeting. Detectives left with what turned out to be a map to the sewer Twitchell had dumped the body in. Finally, the family could have closure. Little did they know Twitchell's defense attorneys were preparing to have him plead to a lesser charge; he had simply improperly disposed of a dead body.

At 5:25 p.m. on Tuesday, April 12, 2011, Mark Andrew Twitchell was charged with the First Degree Murder of John Altinger. It only took the jury five hours to decide his fate. Their decision left the judge with no choice in sentencing; Twitchell would receive an automatic maximum life sentence. As per Canadian law, their deliberations will always remain secret and the six men and six women will have to learn how to live with the burden that silence brings since in Canada jurors remain anonymous and the court employs measures to conceal their identities. That said, in what was called "a rare move," Justice Clackson offered counseling services to each of them, saying that they had seen and heard some very difficult things, often repeated over and over again. But it was all for the greater good! As Detective Clark opined, "We caught a serial killer on his first kill"; Clark said he had no doubt whatsoever that Mark Twitchell would have killed again.

I wasn't able to attend the final verdict because of obligations with my son, but Detective Clark texted me the verdict immediately once he heard them in court. I was so happy about that.

A few hours later, I actually got a call from Detective Clark wanting to tell me the news verbally. I expressed my joy to him over the phone. He then told me that the local media was asking about me and wanted to hear a statement from me. He told me that he probably thought it would be best if I did say something. I agreed with him and he told me that he would set something up.

A few hours went by and received another call from Detective Clark just to let me know that the press conference was set up for the next day, April 13, 2011 at 2:00 p.m., at the Northeast Division Police station. Once I hung up the phone, I got very nervous and thought I better write something down, so I would know what to say the next day. I sat down and wrote from the heart.

The next morning, a few hours before the press conference, I got a call from Detective Clark once again. He told me that he thought we should call the whole thing off. I was a little stunned and asked him why. He said that because my attempted murder charge might still go ahead, they didn't want me talking to the local media at this time. I agreed with him and breathed a sigh of relief because I was a little nervous for the whole thing anyway.

Chapter 27: Moving On

Twitchell's presence haunted my waking and sleeping moments for too many years. I would see him on the street during the day and it would seem as though my darkest nightmares were coming true again. Even though the chances of his escape were minuscule, logic played no part in this. Even knowing that Victims Services would call me immediately if he were to escape, it did not erase my unease. Not his arrest, nor his denied application for bail, nor the impossibility of his escape did anything to stop me from seeing him everywhere I went and imagining the worst case scenario. Although, I saw "him" less and less frequently over the years, he is still following me and I'm not sure when or if I will ever lose him completely.

For the first few years after the attack, the nightmares were daily. Twitchell's dark eyes would peer at me through the protection of his hockey mask causing me to wake in a cold sweat, terrified, my heart beating through my chest. The bad dreams would usually begin with me in the garage, walking in unsuspecting. Then, just like the attack, I would turn around and be surprised to see Twitchell lurched over me. As time went on, I had fewer nightmares about the attack, but to this day, chills run down my back each and every time I think about him or what happened that night. Even though I try not to think about it, every now and then I'll be in the shower or something, and it all comes rushing back. Suddenly, I realize that I should have died that night, and it knocks the wind right out of me.

Detective Clark put Twitchell at the top of the list of killers he has put away in his thirty-year career, having concluded, "he's a psychopathic killer." Knowing that I helped put him behind bars for a very long time was closure enough for me. Victims Services had mentioned that testifying would be a release for me, and they were right. I have been sleeping better and better every night since the verdict. Soon after I told the courtroom my story, a huge weight lifted off my shoulders since I had been holding it in for so long, unable to talk to anyone about the immense stress of it all. After the trial, and the enormous release from testifying, I really did not feel the need to go back to receive therapy from Victims Services. I started the process of moving on through the process of testifying.

Even though they were able to get a direct indictment for both charges, it wouldn't have added any additional jail time if they had charged Twitchell with my attempted murder. The charges were dropped on that charge and I am at peace with the decision not to make Twitchell stand trial for my attempted murder. Not only would my case have added unnecessary monetary costs, the human cost would have been enormous, with the victims having to relive it all over again, including me.

I will admit that I would have loved to see the death penalty as an option in this case. Not that there is another option in Canada than maximum life sentence, but I also agree with John's mother who said, "Twitchell should have to reflect on his actions and die a slow death every day of his life."

Twitchell is now locked away in my home province of Saskatchewan since it houses the closest maximum-security prison. Too many of John Altinger's friends worked at the Edmonton Maximum Security Prison, so Twitchell had to be moved to the nearest prison with a maximum security unit, the Saskatchewan Federal Penitentiary. So, on yet another Friday, April 15, 2011, Twitchell was transferred to his new home. They shackled his wrists to a chain belt which was attached to a metal chair, and that was how he sat for the six-hour drive. A medium security facility with maximum-security areas, the prison is located on twenty acres of penned off land, one kilometer west of Prince Albert, Saskatchewan. In what seems like destiny, the town is home to the original monster of Frankenstein, played by Boris Karloff who stayed in the province for two years and would later go on to gain fame in the 1931 movie. The monster is a character who Twitchell can relate to, since he believed he was just a product of fate, and therefore not responsible for his horrible actions either. In *SKConfessions,* Twitchell freely admits he steals his ideas from fantasy writer, David Gemmell, using his notion of the assassin's "hand of fate,"

When it's their time, it's their time and if they do not die of old age or sickness, when their time comes other factors are employed by fate to get the job done. I think about that whenever I plan a kill. It's not me who chooses the victims but fate. Oh sure I choose the victim to match my own criteria in the interest of remaining free and at large, but for the most part I am merely following my own nature which was devised by the grand design of the universe.

Whether he is a monster of his own creation or one created by the hands of fate, I think he deserves what he's gotten. Twitchell failed creatively and otherwise in life, so he attempted to obtain his spotlight by any means necessary.

There are moments when I worry what Twitchell would try to do to me if he got out of prison in 25, or even 30 years. If he somehow managed to get out immediately when he was able, he would be 54—but he would still be a psychopath! Twitchell moved to Davenport, Iowa in 2001 with his first wife and lived there for four years but moved back to Edmonton after his separation. Part of me wonders if Twitchell's move back to Canada was actually for his career as a serial killer, so that he could avoid a much harsher prison term, or the death penalty. Apparently, he knows that much about our legal system. It's incredibly lax compared to the U.S., and if he were a thinking person, it would make sense to kill in a country, or a province, that allows psychopathic serial killers out of jail.

For instance, Gavin Mandin, from St. Paul, Alberta, killed his mother, stepfather, and two sisters before getting in the car to kill his three cousins. A *true* serial killer, he was caught with the gun and he admitted to it all, showing no remorse, nor feeling the need to try and act as such in court. Now, thirty years later, he is out of jail and walking the streets of the greater Toronto area. An admitted psychopathic killer, he was able to change his name, now living as Gavin McLeod. He is living in a half-way house that requires him to report into at a certain time every night, at least for now. I have it on good authority that some of his family members still live in fear of him, which breaks my heart, and I don't want that for them, or for me in the case of Mark Twitchell.

After the trial was over and done with, I became curious about the fictional character, "Dexter," that Twitchell idolized so much. I decided that I wanted to know what all the fuss was about since I had never read the books or seen the TV show before Twitchell. I was surprised to find myself enjoying the show, but after a few episodes, I had to stop watching it. I didn't mind the violence, but the character reminded me too much of Twitchell.

Despite his deception, Twitchell hasn't left any long-term scars as far as my ability to trust is concerned. In my case, my lack of trust has far more to do with having been divorced. I thought I was going to spend the rest of my life with my ex-wife and when she left, I was devastated. I really didn't see that coming either. As a result, I am doing everything in my power to make sure I don't get blindsided again. I may not have confidence in others as easily as I use to, but it has everything to do with avoiding a second divorce and nothing to do with a maniac in a hockey mask.

After the attack, I began to date a girl named Heather I met through work and we had a son together. Although the relationship didn't last, my son Benjamin is the best thing that has ever happened to me. Born in 2009, he continues to bring me joy on a daily basis. As a father, it's an amazing feeling to know that I am responsible for influencing my son. Whether we know it or not, our sons learn about being a man primarily by watching their fathers. He really challenges me to be the best man I can be so that he can learn to respect women, interact with other people, deal with conflict, among other issues. I'm currently developing common interests with him. I've found that we have bonded playing video games and playing in the park. At his young age, play wrestling is always good. I've noticed with boys, this little bit of wild behavior is a bonding experience. No matter what, I love spending quality time with him and can't wait to see what kind of man he will grow into.

After the trial, I started dating quite a bit due to the attention I was getting in the media. I went on a few dates with women who had seen the programs. I got many friend requests on Facebook after my shows aired and I sometimes took the risk and accepted. I'm a romantic at heart and this whole experience hasn't changed that, but I still managed to get my heart broken.

For instance, I met this woman named Ashley back in December 2012. We had very similar interests since she was from Saskatchewan and was a single parent as well. We finally decided to meet and seemed to hit it off but in the end all she wanted was to visit the actual garage where my attack had taken place and borrow money from me. She had played me good and I knew I would never hear from her again and I would never see that money. This whole feeling had made me quite upset. What kind of person would do that? Did she have any feelings for me at all or did she just admire that I was somewhat famous from what had happened to me? Was she that desperate for money that she used the fact that I liked her so much against me? I guess I will never know but that did teach me a very good lesson. I truly believe in karma and what goes around, comes around. I guess being on television does have a downside. That's when it hit me like a ton of bricks and I decided that I no longer wanted to date a woman that had seen me on television.

Believe it or not, even after all that, I still went on online dating sites, including Plenty of Fish, even after the trial. I wasn't on them as often, however, because I sometimes got a flashback when I was on the dating site. I strongly believe the sites themselves are not to be blamed for what happened to me. I always tell people, "Don't blame the website! If anything, blame the psycho on the other end because he's the one you have to worry about!" As long as you are being safe and meeting people in a public place, I feel online dating is a good way to meet someone. If you choose to meet someone from a dating site, you must follow some simple but effective precautions. Take your time and talk to a woman for quite a while before meeting her. Exchange pictures and talk on the phone prior to ever meeting. If you happen to click over email and the phone, meet in a public place for a coffee or something equally limited in time. If you don't like the person, you only have to spend an hour together, at most. If the date goes well, you can take it longer or you can plan on meeting again for a bit of a longer date. People can be difficult to get to know, so take your time. There's no need to hurry where love is concerned.

Over the years, the fear that ran through my veins was diminishing, thanks to testifying and then writing copious feelings and facts about my ordeal. Everyone has their own way of coping and for me, it is writing. Once I began exploring what happened to me on paper, it was like another weight was lifted off of my shoulders. I was happy to have found a new coping mechanism, and this book is the result. The more I wrote, the more I was able to deal with the trauma. I hoped it could all be for the better good and that I really was alive for a reason and maybe someone could learn from my story, or so I have hoped.

My testimony helped me to move on and it also helped prove the veracity of Twitchell's diary, *SKConfessions*. The theory was: if my part was true then the part about John had to be true as well. My story was very close to what he wrote and I still can't understand why he would write down everything exactly the way it happened with me and then lie about the next part.

In the end, I am elated that I could help put John's murderer and my attempted murderer in jail for a very long time. I have to think of things in a positive light. There are a lot of "what ifs" about this case, and I choose to focus on the positive. If I were to focus on feeling guilty about not coming forward right away, it would only lead to more guilt and sadness. Instead, I chose to focus on the fight for my life and getting away not once but twice. Being "the one who got away" has taught me just how precious each moment is, because I truly know how lucky I am to be alive!

"If you ask me how I want to be remembered, it's as a winner. You know what a winner is? A winner is somebody who has given his best effort, who has tried the hardest they possibly can, who has utilized every ounce of

energy and strength within them to accomplish something. It doesn't mean that they accomplished it or failed, it means that they've given it their best. That's a winner."

-Walter Payton

Appendix 1 – Timeline of Events

2008

August 15
• Mark Twitchell's Facebook profile states, "Mark has way too much in common with Dexter Morgan."

August 27
• A casting call goes out on the website www.mandy.com for actors to star in a movie called *House of Cards*.

August 29
• Somebody living at 30 Dayton Crescent (Twitchell's home address) orders an 800,000 volt stun baton online.

August 31
• Twitchell installs an IP blocker on his computer. An IP blocker is software designed to block anyone from tracing where an email was sent from.

September 3
• Twitchell updates his Facebook profile to state, "Mark feeds on the souls of his defeated foes."

September 28
• Filming is completed for Twitchell's psychological thriller, *House of Cards*, in the garage he is renting.

October 3
• Gilles Tetreault gets attacked by Twitchell but escapes alive. He does not report the attack to the police.

October 10
• John Altinger disappears after telling his friends he's on his way to meet a woman he met from the Plenty of Fish dating website.

October 12
• Twitchell uses Altinger's key to break into his apartment and changes his Facebook status from "Single" to "In A Relationship" and changes status to state, "John is taking off to the Caribbean for a few months. See you all when I get back. Wondering why anyone would leave sun and surf to come home to snow and stress."

• Altinger's friend and co-worker, Hans-Wilhelm Adam, emails Altinger to tell him that he's looking for condos in his area and that he hopes once he buys a condo in his neighbourhood that they can carpool to work together.

October 13
• Hans-Wilhelm Adam gets a reply from Altinger's account stating: "No car pool for me. I'm taking an extended vacation. Good luck."

• Altinger's friends receive a separate Facebook message that states: "Hey there, I've met an extraordinary woman named Jen who has offered to take me on a nice, long tropical vacation. We'll be staying in her winter home in Costa Rica, phone number to follow soon. I won't be back in town till December 10 but I will be checking my email periodically. See you around the holidays. Johnny."

• Altinger's employer at Argus Machine receives an email from Altinger stating, "I quit. I'm going on an extended leave."

October 14
• William Stanic (Altinger's friend and co-worker) tells Hans-Wilhelm Adam that "something is not right" about Altinger's emails and him not showing up for work.

October 17
• Twitchell saves SKConfessions on his computer at 5:17 P.M. In his letters later to the fifth estate Twitchell claims that SKConfessions was the manuscript for a novel. During his trial, the prosecutors argued it was in fact his diary.

• Altinger's friends Dale Smith and Marcel and Carolyn Souza break into Altinger's apartment and find his suitcase, toothbrush and passport still there.

• The friends file a missing person report. They had contacted the police earlier in the week but the police didn't take them seriously.

October 19
• Det. Mike Tabler interviews Twitchell and tells him that Altinger had texted a friend and told him that he had met a man inside of the garage that Twitchell is renting. This is the first time Twitchell learns that Altinger had told someone else that he had met a man inside of Twitchell's garage.

• At some point after he leaves the interview, Twitchell emails Tabler and says that he had forgotten to say it earlier but in fact he had bought a red Mazda (same make as Altinger's car) off of a lady for $40.00. The EPS doesn't learn about this email because by then Tabler is on holiday.

• Twitchell meets with Det. Brian Murphy later that day and tells him about buying the red Mazda. Murphy phones Anstey and that's when they are convinced this is a murder and the case becomes a homicide investigation. They ask Twitchell to go to the EPS station for an interview.

• Twitchell goes to the EPS station and writes out an eight-page statement.

October 20
• Det. Bill Clark interviews Twitchell at 2:00 A.M. He releases Twitchell but confiscates his car.

• Twitchell is put on 24-hour surveillance as soon as he leaves the police station.

October 22
• Police obtain four search warrants: for Twitchell's car, Altinger's car, the garage, and Twitchell's home in St. Albert.

• Constable Mike Roszko goes to Twitchell's home and confiscates his computer and finds part of SKConfessions (30 of the 42 pages) from it, hands the document over to lead detective Mark Anstey.

• This is the first time police learn that there was a second victim who escaped.

October 24
• Police publicly confirm they suspect foul play in Altinger's disappearance.

October 27
• Twitchell writes on his Facebook profile, "Dexter feels the dark passenger getting restless again."

October 31
• Mark Twitchell is arrested in Altinger's murder in front of his parents' house by a team of police officers.

November 1
• Police make a public appeal for the second victim to contact the police.

November 2
• Gilles Tetreault contacts police and tells them he's the first victim.

November 3
• Police interview Gilles Tetreault. His story lines up with what's written in SKConfessions.

November 5
• Det. Dale Johnson, armed with SKConfessions, inspects manholes near Twitchell's parents home for Altinger's body.

November 21
• Twitchell served with divorce papers while he is still in custody in the Edmonton Remand Centre.

December 3
• Twitchell's lawyer enters a plea of not guilty on his behalf in an Edmonton courtroom.

2009

August 20
• Crown prosecutor Lawrence Van Dyke files a rare application for a direct indictment against Mark Twitchell, skipping over the preliminary hearing.

• Crown's office won't comment on why they filed the application but during this period ABC 20/20 is in town gathering information and media speculation is that prosecutors fear trial information covered by the publication ban will be broadcast by U.S. networks seen locally.

September 4
• Crown prosecutors win their application for a direct indictment of Mark Twitchell and the move eliminates Twitchell's right to a preliminary hearing.

September 9
• Det. Bill Clark and Det. Brad Mandrusiak visit Twitchell in the remand centre. They try to persuade Twitchell to give up the location of Altinger's body.

September 18
• A judge denies media access to a series of search warrants that homicide investigators used to collect evidence against Twitchell.

• Assistant Chief Judge James Wheatley also issues a blanket publication ban on the information.

2010

June 3
• Twitchell requests a meeting with the police, specifies he doesn't want Det. Bill Clark there. Det. Brad Mandrusiak goes with Det. Jeff Kerr and meets with Twitchell and his lawyer.

• Twitchell hands Mandrusiak a piece of paper, he opens it once he's left the meeting and it states "Location of John Altinger's remains" and gives directions.

• Mandrusiak goes to the location and sees what he thinks are human remains in the sewer. He doesn't have the equipment to remove the body so he returns the next day.

June 4
• Johnny Altinger's body is recovered from sewer near Twitchell's parents' home.

2011

March 16
• Twitchell's murder trial begins.

April 1
• Gilles Tetreault testifies at Twitchell's murder trial.

April 12

• Twitchell convicted for first degree murder, sentenced to the mandatory 25 years in prison.

May 9
• Twitchell files an appeal of his conviction.

June 17
• Charges stayed in attempted murder charges against Twitchell in attack on Gilles Tetreault.

2012

November 13
• Edmonton police refuse to give back amateur films that were seized during the 2008 homicide investigation to killer Mark Twitchell.

February 15
• Alberta Justice confirmed Twitchell abandoned his appeal and filed notice to that effect.

Appendix 2 – Detective Clark Interview

TRANSCRIPT OF AN INTERVIEW
Between Detective B. CLARK & Gilles TETREAULT
On 2008 November 03
At Edmonton Police Services Headquarters

File #08-137180

(Background noise)
Elapsed time 00:00:37

CLARK   (Door opens and closes) Okay. Uh what I want you to do Gilles is just uh basically walk me through everything

TETREAULT   Okay.

CLARK   and I'll what I'll do is I'll just let you ramble on I might write a few things down, I might not.

TETREAULT   Okay.

CLARK   Urn just

TETREAULT   (Unintelligible) (Overtalk)

CLARK   I want you to start right at the beginning

TETREAULT   Yeah.

CLARK   from any first contact

TETREAULT   Yeah.

CLARK   how it developed. All that type of stuff.

TETREAULT   Okay.

CLARK   And uh then I'll probably have some questions in a

TETREAULT   Okay.

CLARK   you know for you afterwards urn just take your time.
TETREAULT   Alright.
CLARK   We got as long as it takes.
TETREAULT   For sure.
CLARK   There's not rush here so.
TETREAULT   Alright.
CLARK   Start right at the beginning.
TETREAULT   Okay. Uh beginning urn I'm on the Plenty of Fish website. Plenty of Fish dot com. That's where I met this girl urn I believe I made the first contact. Uh just because I saw the picture, her picture. She looked you know attractive looking, I have pictures of her, I believe I sent them, I emailed them to you guys already but urn... and uh we started talking urn this probably was... I'm guessing around September, end of September. September thirtieth or something like that. There was a couple maybe three four days before I actually met her. And I just talked to her, almost every single day before the encounter. So urn we had chatted and urn she was pretty forward I thought uh uh actually cuz uh like I I remember her saying something like... what are you doin' Friday or somethin' like that. And I said oh, well do you wanna meet. Is that you know is that what you're getting at. She's like well I'm thinkin' about it. And so urn we started talkin' about that and then we started (stammers) I can't I said well what do you wanna do or somethin' like that and then she basically said how well how 'bout urn... uh (stammers) somethin' about uh she didn't wanna eat the junk food at the movie theatre so how 'bout we we go to a restaurant first. And and then go to the movies. And I thought that was a great idea so you know. Cuz she we had made plans to go to I believe I don't know Edmonton that well, but I believe she said South Common.

Is uh I guess there's I've never really been there but is I guess there's a Joeys restaurant there and then right beside there (stammers) there's supposed to be a movie theatre. Urn and so we had made plans to do that. And urn she (stammers) I said okay well give me your phone number or cell number you know so we can you know talk or whatever. Urn set this up. And she would never give me any numbers, and I thought (stammers) I thought it was really odd. And so she's like uh you know she basically kept saying it was for security reasons you know basically she didn't wanna give her information out in case you know I was a stalker or something right. So I knew I understood that urn so (stammers) I ss- uh she finally gave me these directions which I have here as well.

CLARK   Okay.

TETREAULT   They were pretty urn well (sighs) first of all the I like (stammers) she asked me where I was from, where I lived like cl•uh what road I was closed to and I said uh Fort Road, and the directions (stammers) I don't know he got mixed up and (stammers) gave me directions from Groat Road. So he sent me these directions and I'm like whoa okay well that's way down the south end so I kinda found my own directions which I have printed out here. And I kinda figured out where she, she where she what she was talking about. So I said I think I know where I'm going but you know I may get lost I I don't know the city that well like maybe you should give me your cell number or a phone number that I can call in case I get lost and I can't find this place. Because these directions she gave me seemed really odd to me. And then then she she but she... she made it uh sound like that was the only way is that you know (stammers) you go she (stammers) had these directions she said you have to go to the back alley you have to park at the back cuz that's where the the driveway is. You know and you have to park there and the way this house is made you have to go through the garage, that's the only way and it's uh I'm renting this house and so urn (stammers) my door is at the back of the house and you have to urn knock at the back of the door. And I thought that's kinda odd too but you know whatever I didn't know the house, I didn't know the place and she said I'll leave the garage door open a little bit for you so that you can get in. And uh you know (stammers) I thought it was kinda odd but you know you just

CLARK   Yeah.

TETREAULT   I wasn't really thinkin' about it it seemed pretty urn convincible you know.

CLARK   Right.

TETREAULT   So I thought okay okay. Urn... (stammers) we'll try this okay. So urn... but uh uh everyday up to that I kept asking for a number or something she wouldn't give it to me so. So fine okay I'll go do this. So Friday comes along, we set it up, she set it up for seven p.m. Urn I (stammers) I was an idiot cuz I I I I finish work at six, so I realize that day I'm like oh my God, I'm not gonna make it on time, and she basically said in our email be sure you're on time. So I urn I said oh great I'm gonna be late. And so cuz had I to rush home from work, change and then go uh uh drive all the way down to the south end. And uh so I'm driving and driving uh to this place. Urn and uh I'm in a rush because I don't wanna be late (stammers) but I (stammers) it happens that I am late, so I'm like fifteen minutes late. But finally find the place actually that the directions like she gave was okay. I (stammers) I was able to find it (stammers) pretty well. So urn I find this back alley I yeah sure enough the door is open, a little ways. And urn I'm in this rush because I think I'm late. And so I uh I get outta my truck, and urn I kinda rush to the garage not really thinking like I should'a been maybe scopin' out the garage a little before yeah... but cuz I'm late I'm like oh God I gotta go and and so as soon as I went to the other side of the garage I went open (stammers) to open the door, he came from behind and grabbed me. And I'm like holy... what the hell's goin' on. And um he came after me with uh he grabbed me and then he was had this uh, at the time I thought it was like Taser or um um cattle prod type gun thing. Um I uh now that I watched the news I see it's probably the stun gun and it it looks it looked like that. So um it every time he pressed the trigger it turned blue. And um he's hitting me all over with this stun gun. And um it's not hurting me. And I'm just like thinking what the hell is this idiot and then I turn around finally and I see this guy and he's wearing this mask and that just freaked me out. And I knew it was no joke right at that point.

CLARK   Right.

TETREAULT   So then um I (stammers) at this he's still tazering me or whatever and so it's not hurting me and I'm Like jeez what what is this thing and so I just grabbed it and I cuz I didn't want him tapering my body so he was but he kept triggering it and he was tazering my hand, but it felt like uh you know one of those mosquito zappers. And so um I'm like uh are you kidding me you're trying to hurt me with this thing. Right. And it so it wasn't hurting me but now that I think about it, it probably weakened me, and it drained me and I was off balance. So um... he uh finally he let we let go. He knew he couldn't do anymore cuz I was holding on to that thing and he was triggering triggering triggering and he couldn't do anything more so finally put it away um I can't remember in the shuffle... he uh finally put it away but then he pulled out his gun. He had um uh it was a (stammers) a little handgun IJm it in the garage it was (stammers) very dark uh it was seven o'clock at night, or seven fifteen at night so it was still kinda light out like and so there was light coming in but inside this garage it was fairly dark. So when he pulled the gun out I could not tell if it was a real gun. Urn... fake gun I it was too far away uh so at this point I wh- was scared for my life basically I thought I was gonna die at at this point. So he urn he yelled to me urn get down on the ground, put your face down, put your hands behind your back. And urn basically (stammers) in my head I figured I'd better do what he says because he has this gun and I don't know like I don't know it could be real so I didn't what he told me to. So urn uh I did that and he kept uh I kept kinda lookin' up to see what he'd be doing and he kept shouting yelling at me to not close my eyes and and look down. So I was kinda doin' that but you know I still kind've had one eye lookin'. Urn that's when he uh pulled duct tape out and urn cut a piece and he put it over my eyes. So I have a lot of stuff goin' on in my head, I don't know, I think I'm gonna die, I I basically I believe at this point I told him I started talkin' to him I said just take what you want, I'll give you anything you want, just let me go. He responds back, yeah if you cooperate this is just gonna be a standard robbery. So urn we (stammers) he continues all of a sudden I hear urn his belt jiggling, he's jiggling somethin' in his belt, trying to... grabbing somethin' I can't see what it what he's doin'. I don't know what he's doin'. I think I thought he was gonna tie me up. Tie my hands up. I uh but I have a whole lot of stuff goin' on in my head, and when I heard the belt jiggling, I thought maybe he was urn well a couple things, I thought he (stammers) he might kill me. Or he might or he was going to rape me. I really thought that. So I'm down on the ground, he hasn't done anything to my hands yet. I still have 'em (stammers) behind (stammers) my back. And I'm thinkin' okay... II can't go down like this, this is not the way II don't know what's gonna happen, I'm don't know where what he's gonna do to me. I can't go down like this. So basically somehow for some reason, I decided to take the chance and... fight this guy. So (stammers) I he hadn't tied my hands yet, I rip off the tape, off my eyes, I stand up. That got him very very angry. Um he kept telling me go down, get (stammers) back down, get back down. And I wouldn't do it. And I basically when I got up I told him, I yelled back at him, I said I'm not goin' down like this. And he really wasn't happy that I did that. So um... (sighs) at this point I'm face to face with him again, I'm much closer to him this time. He pulls this gun out... again. Because I'm closer to him this time I'm able to see well... it still looked okay (stammers) I was able to see the gun a little better. And to me, here's the things that were going in my head, I said okay, (stammers) I don't think it's a real gun.   It could be a BB gun or a pellet gun. Water gun. But it really doesn't look like a real gun to me. So I said, in my head I'm like okay if it's a BB gun or a pellet gun it's not really hurt me right now I'm I'm high on adrenaline. Um if it's a real gun I'm gonna take my chances, so basically I I was thinkin' uh (stammers) um this is all this stuff's goin' through my head and I'm goin' okay if it's a real gun I gotta grab the gun and then maybe I can steer it in the direction I want in case he fires and then it's not gonna hit me. And uh and then I can wrestle with him and maybe escape. So that's what I decide to do. I actually grab the end of the gun... and um... ha (laughs)... I I keep ha (laughs)...I keep telling my friends this uh it was the best feeling I ever felt (laughs) cuz I felt plastic. And then I knew it wasn't real gun and so um I was pretty hyped up on adrenaline so I was uh trying to break the gun... with my bare hand. And I actually hurt my hand, it's uh (stammers) um doing it. Um he was getting mad. Because... he didn't want me touchin' his gun I guess. Obviously and try and breaking it. Um... so uh we wrestle for a little bit um I'm tryin' to break this gun I don't know how Long maybe uh a minute or two or somethin' tryin' to break the gun. Um he never ever once fired it so I obviously in my head said this is a fake gun. While we're doin' that I look down... and there's a pair of handcuffs on the ground. And um I know handcuffs, like I work at security so I looked at the handcuffs they were heavy metal uh they were black... and uh they it was like the police type handcuffs they can lock. I believe I uh I (laughs) cuz at that point I I uh uh once I saw the handcuffs, see I didn't know he was gonna handcuff me, I thought he was just gonna tie me up. And when I saw the handcuffs I flew off the handle, cuz I'm like this is no standard robbery now. So I knew at this point it was just a fake gun, so I let the gun go cuz I knew it couldn't hurt me anymore. So then I go and pick up his handcuffs, well that sent him off the handle again. Cuz he didn't want me havin' his handcuffs. And (stammers) I think they're pretty expensive handcuffs too, that's my opinion though. But uh so I'm (stammers) have his these handcuffs in my in my fist, and I'm I'm willin' to start hitting him with them. Cuz it's all I had but he (stammers) kept yelling at me yelling put the handcuffs down, put the handcuffs down. And at this point I thought okay, even if I hit him with the handcuffs I I can't it's not really gonna do much so why frustrate this guy more, I might as well just fight him off myself bare fisted or barehanded and just let go of the handcuffs. But basically I didn't wanna let the handcuffs go that easy so I threw 'em in the corner of the garage. Uh he was (stammers) upset with that. Uh but not much he can do cuz he couldn't go get 'em or anything. So urn... that's when urn... and he grabbed me and uh we were kinda shuffling all over the place again, wrestling a little bit uh but then uh wrestling standing up, and that's when he head-bunted me with the facemask he but (stammers) it caught me off guard cuz he hit me in the head right right about here. Urn but luckily he didn't hit me hard enough to to knock me unconscious or anything he just it was a little bit of painful it was like whoa holy crap he's fighting dirty now right. So urn so I kept uh I basically I I uh in my head I'm like I better I gotta ss- now watch for this him head-bunting me. And so I gotta keep my head away from his face. Urn... so... (sighs) I I believe at this point he says something like urn... I think it was somethin' like uh uh because you're not cooperating this is the way it has to be. And I didn't answer him I'm like whatever and so then uh then he starts punching me. And he uh... he punched me a couple of times but (stammers) the first time he caught me he got me around the temple here. Um... pretty uh I remember thinkin' is pretty hard, he was fairly strong. And um but he (stammers) I remember then I remember thinking okay okay he punched me I think again, whatever. It wasn't really hurting me at the time. Um obviously cuz I'm pretty high on adrenaline again, um but um... he uh... oh that's when I figured okay see I that whole time I'm thinking in my head how am I gonna escape. And um... after once he started punching me... I figured out that hey I can maneuver myself where in the position I want. So uh so I can escape. So basically that's what I did. I let him punch me cuz I could have probably protected myself or stopped him. I let him punch me a couple times. And I (stammers) I maneuver myself in exactly kinda where I wanted, and um II forgot to mention that I I'm wearing um this light black summer jacket. Is an Old Navy jacket. Uh very thin uh you didn't zipper it up or anything. Um and so then my whole plan the whole time was basically I know I can slip out of this jacket fairly easy. I just need to (stammers) make sure he has a good hold on my jacket. That's what happened. So I maneuver myself where I wanted. He had a nice grip on my jacket. I knew I saw the door. I knew it was perfect time I had to try to escape. That's what I did. So I uh slipped out of the jacket. Um... ran under the door. Um got outside and I (stammers) I I believe I remember thinking thank God I'm out of this garage but um for some reason and (stammers)... makes sense now but at the time I thought I was just so weak because of the struggling I've been struggling with the guy for about twenty twenty-five minutes now. So I'm thinking I'm weak cuz of that but now that I look think back now and see that it's probably the stun gun. I was all off balance, I couldn't run, I couldn't... so then I uh I (laughs) I couldn't run I I fell down on the the gravel driveway and uh basically crawling. I could not hardly get up. And uh and I'm (stammers) this is right beside my truck at this time. So obviously he comes right after me. And I'm like oh my God because I'm thinking in my head if he catches me again and he brings me back in this garage I don't know how I'm gonna escape this again because I'm out of ideas. So um he does grab me... starts dragging me back but as he's dragging me back there's this nice size rock, I try to grab the rock it just slipped out of my hands but uh if I would'a grabbed that rock I would've probably hit him in the head with it. But I didn't I I couldn't get on a hold of this rock. So then he drags me back to the garage. Now I don't remember all that happened after this but all now that I think about it like I I was thinking about it last night and basically I think what happened is because the garage door was a little lower he had to also get underneath it and drag me underneath. So he couldn't he had to let me go at one point. Cuz I was able to escape again, uh at that point. Urn and so that's the only I don't remember how I did it, but I believe that's why he had to let me go so he can get under the garage. So then I escaped again. This time I have a Little more um energy, I can actually (stammers) run or maybe jog more of a jog. (stammers) I'm I'm running down this this the back alley... and I (stammers) for some reason there's this walking path right beside the place and uh coincidentally there's a couple.

CLARK   Mmhm.

TETREAULT   Happen to be there walkin' their dog. Um I uh for some reason he didn't come after me right away. And it took him a bit to come after me. Urn my best guess is that he went to grab his handcuffs that I threw in the corner. I'm not sure though. So at this point I see this couple and I knew just having that couple there that it would help me greatly and I didn't have to run anymore. Cuz that would deter him. He didn't want anyone uh to see him. And um... once I met this couple I (laughs) I was so out of breath Ill was kinda leaning lower and I ju- I'm sure they were scared of me but I I basically said there's a guy attacking me I I (stammers) don't quote me on it here but I but something like II there's a guy attacking me, he's trying mug me, please help me for something like that. And they're just looking at me like stunned. Like what the hells goin' on. And uh sure enough he does come after me again but this time he's uh he's still wear or he's still wearing this his mask, which looks stupid and it's still light out, and these guys or this this couple sees him with this hockey mask on. And uh he knows he looks stupid and and so um I believe he yells out something like... huh like he was pretending to be my best friend, it was just all a joke. And uh something like... hey hey Fred or something like that or... hey friend or something like that. And I I oh and then when he came out but actually before that sorry um to the couple I yelled out that's the man. Or that's the guy. And then that's when he did oh Fred or friend and he then he looked (stammers) he pretended like he was gonna pull up his hockey mask and that but he turned around right away. And then he started walking back to the garage. The couple... then decided to leave (laughs) just (stammers) decide to walk away and uh I've just been struggling with this guy twenty-five minute twenty-five yeah probably about twenty-five minutes and I'm like (stammers) aren't you gonna help me out. And urn... the the (stammers) the guy out of the couple starts walking back and uh but his girlfriend calls his name or calls him back, so he starts walking back to his girlfriend or wife or somethin'. And then I said well at least help me get to my vehicle like just just stay (stammers) just stay here, watch me try to get to my truck, and and so I can get home (stammers) uh get into it safely. He comes back and his wife girlfriend calls him back again he walks away. So basically I don't know if they heard me but I basically I I said okay fine I'll do it myself. And then uh I knew at this point I I still... uh pretty smart I I knew at this point that he I had the advantage cuz he he didn't see the couple walk away. And he um he probably thought I was still with them. So I knew I had the advantage so then I decided I could probably I can run and get away I can follow the couple I could uh run on the street maybe get to house, flag a car down. Then I thought in my, in this case, it's best if 1... he thinks I'm with this couple, I'm gonna go back by myself... which is stupid now that I think about it. But I'll go back by myself.

CLARK   Mmhm.

TETREAULT   Get into my truck and lock the doors, even if he comes out he has to break the windows to get to me. So I go I do go back. And then I see him uh (stammers) I see his feet under the garage door, pacing back and forth in the garage. Um and then I see my jacket in on the floor still laying on the floor. And I'm thinking man I'd love to get my jacket back (laughs) for some stupid I'm not thinking straight. So then uh but I thought no no my jackets not worth my life so okay so... so then urn I that's what exactly what I did. I I unlocked the door. I get in my truck. Lock both doors. Start the truck. Get and get outta there. Urn... so basically I escape, that's how I escaped (stammers) uh I tried I I started driving home, and I was still high on adrenaline, and um I got maybe half way home and then I I was starting to come down on the adren— rush. And everything that happened and um I started hurting bad by side of the face, and my chest uh cuz I um I don't when or where or what maybe but basically I think he kneed me in the the chest. Uh... just paining and I just couldn't drive anymore or on so I pulled over to the side and and um I felt like throwing up but I couldn't throw up and (stammers) exhausted and urn couldn't drive, couldn't do anything. Urn... not thinking straight, didn't call anybody. I had a cell phone on me didn't, I could'a called the cops I didn't think of that either. Just wasn't thinking. So t en uh... I decided to lay down in my truck for a while, I don't know how long. And then I I get back up uh and I had some water in my truck, drank some water um and then I uh finally I think I think I can get home. So then I drive away. And I finally do get home. I pass out on my bed for a couple hours. Um in pain. Uh then urn I wake up and then I think about what's happened and... I thought you know what I better try to get as much information as I can, go back on the website and and... get everything. And I go back and this may be two hours later. And everything's gone. The profiles gone, the sent and received messages that we sent were all completely vanished, gone. Urn and so uh whatever I have here is is all that I have.

CLARK   Okay.

TETREAULT   That's pretty much it. Uh II put some cold compresses on my face. The swelling went down. Urn I had a kind of a he didn't hit me in the the uh cuz he hit me in the temple I had a black eye on the side for a couple weeks urn... for about two weeks my chest hurt I think my rib was out or bruised or something. Urn I'm fine now. I'm okay now but...

CLARK   Okay. That's quite the story. It's amazing it's... I guess you realize how lucky you were.

TETREAULT   I that I thought I was... after this all happened I realize how lucky I was. But not until now... it's so much bigger.

CLARK   Yeah. And you know what and I appreciate it's it's hard for you to to relive it.

TETREAULT   Yeah.

CLARK   I can see it in in in the way

TETREAULT   I get shivers down

CLARK   yeah I can see

TETREAULT   my back.

CLARK   I can see it, but you know what I appreciate your honesty and that's all I'm here for, I'm not here to judge you.

TETREAULT   No.

CLARK   Don't get me wrong.

TETREAULT   No that's fine.

CLARK   I'm just here to get the information and urn we need to put this guy away

TETREAULT   I I agree.

CLARK   for a long time. And we really appreciate you coming forward

TETREAULT   No

CLARK   cuz it's so important to this investigation but urn yeah it's, it's it's

TETREAULT   I don't know what he would'a

CLARK   just a bizarre

TETREAULT   done to me

CLARK   situation.

TETREAULT   like

CLARK   The whole thing you know.

TETREAULT   uh yeah II thought you know what my in my head I thought (stammers) after I seen the tape and the handcuffs I I basically though he wasn't... going to mug me he was gonna take me somewhere. That's my first impression is that he's gonna do something to me. It sure wasn't to take my money. Urn then uh no things when you think back on it like if the couple would'a helped me out. I had him cornered in the garage and I knew I knew in my head that is not his garage like cuz he didn't go into the house didn't go in the backyard, he stayed in that damn garage. So thinking back on it if the couple would've helped me and called the cops, we could probably could'a caught him at that time. But you know who knows what he might'a done, maybe he would've attacked all three of us, uh you know and you never know. And and urn in the struggle... I thought I felt a urn I don't know what it was (stammers) in my head though I felt this is a... some kind of pouch hanging from his belt and I thought oh my God he has a knife on him but he never did pull it out. don't know... it might've been for his other (stammers) gun or his Taser or or whatever it is. I don't know.

CLARK   Okay.

TETREAULT   But I felt that and then it just scared me that he might have a knife on him as well. He was uh he was anyway and then urn I think thought back on it all now and is was very he set me up very well it was all very properly setup and I knew that. I knew that right from as soon as I got back.

CLARK   Okay urn I'm just gonna take you through it again

TETREAULT   Sure.

CLARK   I have a bunch of questions to ask

TETREAULT   For sure.

CLARK   just to clarify some things urn... things that we're gonna need to check up on and stuff like that.

TETREAULT   Okay.

CLARK   Starting with urn... well first of all what day did all this happen to you?

TETREAULT   The day? October third.

CLARK   October third.

TETREAULT   Yeah. I I urn I thought it wasn't and then I took a look cuz I printed this out on the day of. There you go, October third.

CLARK   You printed this map and this is the map (overtalk)

TETREAULT   Yeah this is the (overtalk)

CLARK   of basically how to (overtalk)

TETREAULT   basically here's the directions he gave me. And urn from the directions on my own okay where it's what's what's goin' on here so then I basically said okay what do I need to do from my house uh to get to this place. So... oh... yeah here so basically I said I can go down Wayne Gretzky Drive. Go down Whyte Ave to uh I think it was Fiftieth. Yeah Fiftieth. Go all the way down and then once I get to Fiftieth just turn on Fortieth

CLARK   Ave.

TETREAULT   Ave right here and and then uh from the directions I could probably find where it is.

CLARK   Okay what I'll get you to do is just use that table just sign your name there.

TETREAULT   Oh sure okay.

CLARK   Cuz I'm gonna need to keep that okay.

TETREAULT   Okay no problem. And uh... yeah... here's the other stuff.

CLARK   Okay and the other stuff you have?

TETREAULT   The other stuff um basically we were emailing back and forth and she had emailed me the directions so and I didn't um I knew I wouldn't remember so I copied it and pasted it into a text uh document (clears throat) and this is exactly his words. He used. And uh the first part anyway, that was the first part. Then a couple a day or two later I kept asking him about it I said are you sure I gotta through this garage and you know it doesn't seem right and and then that's when he says yeah I said it's and it's that to the backdoor of the house, he says yeah yeah yeah just go through the back (unintelligible) and that's why he (stammers) put yeah first visible backdoor coming out of the garage, knock away. Uh uh to the house right. There's uh certainly no other driveways along the alley like this one and a half open car door a dead giveaway see you at seven on Friday. And I said okay. And that was the day before follow it.

CLARK   Okay I'll just get you to sign all
(overtalk)
TETREAULT   Oh sure thing. Um I wrote down here
cuz I had trouble remembering the uh the actual user name
he was using and it was Spiderwebzz he was using that
name.
CLARK   Spiderwebzz?
TETREAULT   Webs with a Z Z.
CLARK   W.E.B.Z.Z.
TETREAULT   Yeah that's the actual (overtalk)
CLARK   Spiderwebzz.
TETREAULT   user name he was using. Um and
then once we got to know each other he started going
Sheena.
CLARK   Sheena?
TETREAULT   Right.
CLARK   And what's the other paper you got?
TETREAULT   And the other paper is just the
pictures off of the website, that he this is the girl that I
thought I was going to meet. These are three pictures on her
profile. And these are the pictures.
CLARK   Okay do you wanna just sign those.
TETREAULT   Sure (Unintelligible)
CLARK   So he was using the name
Spiderwebzz.
TETREAULT   Right.
CLARK   And the person you're you're you're
talking to is spider
TETREAULT   Spiderwebzz.
CLARK   spider and the W.E.B.Z.Z. all one
word.
TETREAULT   All one word. Yeah.
CLARK   And

TETREAULT	That was the
CLARK	when he signed
TETREAULT	user
CLARK	this letter it says
TETREAULT	Yes.
CLARK	uh the the directions it's signed Sheena.
TETREAULT	Sheena.
CLARK	S.H.E.E. TETREAULT She finally gave
CLARK	N.A.
TETREAULT	me her real name supposedly.
CLARK	Yeah.
TETREAULT	Yeah. It was Sheena. And that was the, it was on the profile. All those pictures.
CLARK	Okay what email address do you go by? Or what is your email address?
TETREAULT	For... for uh... my actual email address
CLARK	Yeah.
TETREAULT	you can con—
CLARK	What is your
TETREAULT	Gilles dot
CLARK	okay give it to me again.
TETREAULT	Gilles at Gilles at Tetreault dot org.
CLARK	Gilles at Tetreault dot org.
TETREAULT	Right.
CLARK	Now how long have you been on the Plenty of Fish how long have you been a member of that site?
TETREAULT	Uh probably I I can't remember but it's been a while like probably May
CLARK	May.

TETREAULT   or so back back there. But I haven't
met anyone except for like two girls. And uh urn and it's
this was gonna be the third time I met someone. And the
other two
CLARK   Yeah.
TETREAULT   went fine like it was
CLARK   Yeah.
TETREAULT   nice people right but
CLARK   Well I'm I'm sure that's most
TETREAULT   The the
CLARK   ninety-eight percent of the people
TETREAULT   actual
CLARK   like that.
TETREAULT   site is great.
CLARK   Yeah.
TETREAULT   It's not the sites fault. It's the
CLARK   Yeah.
TETREAULT   site is a very good place to meet
people it's just
CLARK   Yeah.
TETREAULT   there are some sick people out there.
CLARK   Yeah obviously.
TETREAULT   Yeah.
CLARK   Urn so what name do you use when
you when you're conversin' with this
TETREAULT   Yes.
CLARK   with Sheena here
TETREAULT   I I
CLARK   what name
TETREAULT   I was
CLARK   do you use?
TETREAULT   I have two profiles (stammers) and I
have a reason for that but

CLARK   Okay tell tell me about your
TETREAULT   but the one
CLARK   first profile.
TETREAULT   the one profile that I was using with her was (stammers) uh it's called Doctor X but its D.R. underscore X.
CLARK   D.R. underscore
TETREAULT   Underscore.
CLARK   X.
TETREAULT   X.
CLARK   Yeah.
TETREAULT   that's the one I used to converse with her.
CLARK   Profile.
TETREAULT   And then I believe I have a different email for that one as well. So that when people contact me it gets sent to my email address and that's a different email.
CLARK   Okay so which email do you use for that one?
TETREAULT   That one is D.R., how it went, and D.R. underscore X four you number four you at Hotmail dot com.
CLARK   Okay when you're when you're conversing now
TETREAULT   Yeah.
CLARK   With this person, just this one now, not worried
TETREAULT   Yeah.
CLARK   about the other ones.
TETREAULT   Okay
CLARK   All (unintelligible) goes this one.
TETREAULT   Yeah.

CLARK   Urn what name do you, do you ever
use a a full name? Do you ever give your name out like
here uh he signed Sheena?
TETREAULT   Yeah.
CLARK   Did you ever sign your name?
TETREAULT   I can't remember. I might'a.
CLARK   What name would you use though?
TETREAULT   I think I I'd use my real name.
CLARK   You use your real name. You've
never used a fake name?
TETREAULT   I might of uh--
CLARK   Okay what name would you use?
TETREAULT   Sometimes I use uh Brian. Just
because I just I don't want people knowin' my real name
right away sometimes.
CLARK   Right.
TETREAULT   Uh... so I go B.R.I.A.N. Sometimes. I
don't remember in this case. Or or my real name. And
maybe even Paul. That's my middle name but I maybe I
doubt it. I doubt I used that, it probably be Brian or Gilles.
CLARK   Okay but you can't remember for
sure which one
TETREAULT   I cannot.
CLARK   you used. Okay.
TETREAULT   No.
CLARK   (Stammers) any other online names
you use?
TETREAULT   I think I would'a used my real name.
CLARK   'Kay you think (overtalk)
TETREAULT   Yeah
CLARK   you used
TETREAULT   cuz I've actually when I (overtalk)
CLARK   So Gilles

TETREAULT   think I like the girl.
CLARK   G.I.L.L.E.S.?
TETREAULT   Right.
CLARK   Okay. Urn and then (stammers) as far as your profile details did you give any other details of?
TETREAULT   Yeah I did everything like it says it on the website but basically yeah I basically said I'm thirty-three years old, five seven, five eight, hundred and forty pounds. Yeah they (laughs) there's a description on the TV
CLARK   Yeah.
TETREAULT   (unintelligible) (laughs)
CLARK   Yeah.
TETREAULT   But uh urn a hundred and forty pounds, I've short brown hair. Uh green blue eyes. Yeah (laughs).
CLARK   Well yeah there was a reason for that thought but uh
TETREAULT   (unintelligible)
CLARK   I can't really go into that.
TETREAULT   I got'cha. Yeah.
CLARK   Um so the person you're going to see.
TETREAULT   Yeah.
CLARK   What was do you know it was Spiderwebzz?
TETREAULT   Yeah.
CLARK   Just like that.
TETREAULT   Exactly like that.
CLARK   Spiderwebzz where you wrote it down.
TETREAULT   Yeah.
CLARK   And when when did you print this out? This directions.

TETREAULT   I would've printed that out... might've been the same day as the map.

I had I had copied and paste know what no... October second. Because I have an uh the actual thing it says October second I made that file.

CLARK   Okay.

TETREAULT   Yeah. I did it the day before.

CLARK   Okay so, you're talking to Spiderwebzz.

TETREAULT   Mm hm.

CLARK   And then the only other name you got from them was Sheena.

TETREAULT   Right.

CLARK   No contact information no

TETREAULT   Yeah.

CLARK   addresses.

TETREAULT   Just the directions.

CLARK   Is is your communications strictly via this the website? Is 1t all done via the plentyoffish website?

TETREAULT   Right.

CLARK   It's not done on your own emails? Email to email? Everything's through plentyoffish.

TETREAULT   Yeah. Everything. That's why when I went back to get the rest of sent and received messages cuz I'm uh stupid too right I'm thinkin' hey I'll try to get as much information just in case I wanna go to the cops too. And I may copy and paste every every single sent receive message but they were all gone already.

CLARK   Would you have a problem with our tech guys looking at your computer and it's only for this information we don't care what the rest of the stuff is on your computer we just need to pull off anything that had to do with it, what they would do is image your computer would take a day, day and half.

TETREAULT   Okay.

CLARK   And then give it back to you. But it's a fact of they just need to find this information will be on your computer and you know how you say you can't find it.

TETREAULT   Yeah.

CLARK   It's gonna be in there.

TETREAULT   Really?

CLARK   They can pull it off.

TETREAULT   Okay.

CLARK   And we (stammers) really need to do that so we can see how uh we're trying to get the similarities between the two cases here.

TETREAULT   'Kay.

CLARK   Because you got away unfortunately

TETREAULT   Yeah.

CLARK   another guy didn't.

TETREAULT   I know.

CLARK   And we need to this that is huge evidence to show the similarities.

TETREAULT   Okay.

CLARK   So is there a problem if they uh if (overtalk)

TETREAULT   If I can help sure.

CLARK   Okay that's great. So what I'll do is I'll probably arrange that with them today

TETREAULT   Okay.

CLARK   and do you work today or?

TETREAULT   II do though yeah I work at five thirty.

CLARK   Okay.

TETREAULT   But I'm off I work five thirty to three thirty and I'm off all morning all afternoon again tomorrow (overtalk)

CLARK   All tomorrow?

TETREAULT   Yeah.

CLARK   Well okay well we'll probably make arrangements uh

TETREAULT   Done.

CLARK   I'll see what, what they can do and uh it'll like I say I'll only have it for a couple days

TETREAULT   No that's

CLARK   and we'll have it back to you.

TETREAULT   that's fine.

CLARK   So.

TETREAULT   That's fine if I

CLARK   Okay good.

TETREAULT   if I can help out. That's good.

CLARK   Urn... so do you know you said it was around September thirtieth end of September you made the first

TETREAULT   Yeah

CLARK   contact?

TETREAULT   I think it was September thirtieth it was probably three four days before I actually met with her.

CLARK   Okay. And when you say uh

TETREAULT   Maybe September first or--

CLARK   do you remember what time was it like does it say I don't know the website but does it

TETREAULT   Yeah.

CLARK   say on the uh

TETREAULT   Yes it does.

CLARK   website when they're setup?

TETREAULT   Uh it says that when when they sent and receive a message it'll say the time.

CLARK   Okay.

TETREAULT   Exact time.

CLARK   So yours should all be on there.

TETREAULT   Oh sure if you can

CLARK   (Unintelligible)

TETREAULT   get it off of it.

CLARK   Yeah.

TETREAULT   Yeah.

CLARK   They'll probably be able to pull that stuff up so

TETREAULT   I I was hoping that maybe you could contact plentyoffish they would have maybe something.

CLARK   Well we will. Yeah we have, we have to do that through search warrant

TETREAULT   Okay.

CLARK   and all that and that takes months to do.

TETREAULT   Oh.

CLARK   But this way we can

TETREAULT   I got you.

CLARK   get little stuff a little quicker.

TETREAULT   Okay. Okay.

CLARK   But we are doing that too that's something we're gonna do. Um... okay so you mentioned (stammers) the person was pretty forward.

TETREAULT   Yeah.

CLARK   Kinda surprised you about that.

TETREAULT   Yes.

CLARK   Uhh... okay so (Mumbles) did it mention anything about what type of movie or anything you were planning to go see that night?

TETREAULT   Yeah I believe they did. She says yeah I wanna go see this one movie and I can't remember the name for it's in the sent and receive messages though. I don't

CLARK   Okay.

TETREAULT   remember it was some, I remember thinking it's some movie I've never heard of.

CLARK   Okay.

TETREAULT   Oh man I can't remember.

CLARK   No that's fine. Um... now when you go there, you were describing the um... you just basically followed these directions.

TETREAULT   I followed the directions.

CLARK   And did you find (Overtalk)

TETREAULT   And (Unintelligible)

CLARK   it without trouble or did you

TETREAULT   I didn't find

CLARK   have problems?

TETREAULT   no I didn't have a problem at all and all of a sudden I see this garage, yellow doors, the door's part way open and {Stammers) it's exactly

CLARK   Okay.

TETREAULT   like (Stammers) like he said the sofas the crap sofas on the side and the the driveways the only driveway that it's not paved.

CLARK   Okay.

TETREAULT   Exactly like they said.

CLARK   So stand up and tell me how high that garage door is open. On you.

TETREAULT   Oh probably about this high.

CLARK   So about waist high?

TETREAULT   Yeah.

CLARK   So when you go in do have to

167

TETREAULT   I actually
CLARK   actually crawl in?
TETREAULT   I had to urn
CLARK   Or did you--
TETREAULT   go like this. Yeah so maybe a little higher than I'm saying.
CLARK   Okay. You didn't have to get down on your hands and knees?
TETREAULT   No no.
CLARK   You could just kinda
TETREAULT   Yeah kinda I just
CLARK   (Unintelligible)
TETREAULT   went like this kinda.
CLARK   Okay. Okay
TETREAULT   Yeah.
CLARK   good. Now when you go in
TETREAULT   Yeah.
CLARK   describe what you see when you first go in.
TETREAULT   All I remember thinking uh seeing is is dark, I remember seeing some kind of window right (stammers) against the wall. Door to the left hand side. And I know hey that's the door. Um now that I think about it there was like film on top of the windows and stuff like that. Um I all I had on my mind was to get to that door and get into that yard to go knock on the door and that's (stammers) (snapping sound)
CLARK   What was
TETREAULT   goal.
CLARK   the uh what was the plan like was there something ever exchanged in the emails about why you couldn't go the front or why an address wasn't given?
TETREAULT   Yeah.

CLARK   Was that ever
TETREAULT   I kept
CLARK   talked about?
TETREAULT   asking. I kept asking her
CLARK   Right.
TETREAULT   I was like give me your address at least. And she said oh no no I just give you the directions. So well what's the number on the house? And like that's (stammers) whole three four days in advance that's what we've been talking about like like I that's why I'm thinking what the hell's goin' on give me a cell number give me a house number... uh why just directions. And she would never give it (stammers) no for my protections blah blah blah. And like (sighs) well... okay whatever.
CLARK   Viable though.
TETREAULT   Yeah viable. Because
CLARK   Right. Yeah.
TETREAULT   that's what I'm thinkin' is that you know what if I was her and I'm a girl (Stammers) you know I don't wanna give my phone number out to anyone right? She said basically she said in the email um if everything goes well tonight, like after the dinner and (Stammers) the movie and that, then I'll give you my cell number.   I said okay well that sounds fair.
CLARK   Okay. So... yeah you go there
TETREAULT   Yeah.
CLARK   when you walk which door, which overhead door?
TETREAULT   To the right.
CLARK   If you're looking at the garage.
TETREAULT   I'm looking at the garage it was the right hand door.
CLARK   The white hand, the right hand door.

TETREAULT   Yeah.
CLARK   When you go in
TETREAULT   That's where I park
CLARK   uh
TETREAULT   my truck right in front of the door
that was open.
CLARK   You parked it in front of that one?
Okay. So you go into the garage
TETREAULT   Yeah.
CLARK   you're walking
TETREAULT   I'm rushing for the door yeah.
CLARK   like when you say rushing, describe
that to me.
TETREAULT   Uh
CLARK   Are you running are you—
TETREAULT   no no no. Just a quick
CLARK   Quick pace.
TETREAULT   quick pace yeah.
CLARK   And what's what's the plan now
(Stammers)
TETREAULT   I'm just thinking
CLARK   the person told you
TETREAULT   oh God
CLARK   anything about
TETREAULT   because
CLARK   the door
TETREAULT   I'm
CLARK   or
TETREAULT   nervous about meeting this girl for
the first time.
CLARK   Right.
TETREAULT   And that's what I'm thinking about,
oh my God I'm late. I'm meeting this girl for the first time

oh God I gotta hurry kind of thing and so I'm not thinking at all of you know I should've been more aware of my surroundings and what was going on and be a little more careful but I was stupid. (Unintelligible) (overtalk)

CLARK   (Unintelligible) like I said I'm not here to judge you

TETREAULT   Yeah I know

CLARK   don't worry about that.

TETREAULT   I know.

CLARK   I don't want you

TETREAULT   I'm judging myself

CLARK   thinkin'

TETREAULT   (Laughs)

CLARK   And I and I and I appreciate that yeah you Look back on it it's easy

TETREAULT   Yeah.

CLARK   to Look back on it but when

TETREAULT   That's right.

CLARK   you're doing it.

TETREAULT   that's right.

CLARK   You know... and it happens.

TETREAULT   Yeah and he was

CLARK   But when you

TETREAULT   hidden I I don't remember I think there was he was hidden in the corner. By uh the door's to the left and somehow for some reason I didn't even see him there cuz I'm rushing through. And uh I actually had my hand on the handle and then that's when he (Stammers) right behind me boom. And uh--

CLARK   Okay so you you get to the door.

TETREAULT   Yup.

CLARK   Now is there anything else (overtalk)

TETREAULT   There's film on the (overtalk)

CLARK   in the garage?

TETREAULT   Urn you see that I can't remember, I don't remember

CLARK   Okay.

TETREAULT   uh a lot of that. You know I remember thinking this garage is is uh pretty dirty, dusty, old garage urn

CLARK   Mm hm.

TETREAULT   (Stammers) I can't remember I thought it might been a... a wooden chair in the corner I don't remember. But I cannot I don't know cuz at that point my whole after he (stammers) he urn grabbed me my whole thinking was I gotta survive I gotta stay alive I gotta you know

CLARK   Yeah that survival mode kicks in.

 TETREAULT   Yeah.

CLARK   When you so you walk in, you you go for the door

TETREAULT   Yeah.

CLARK   do you turn it or?

TETREAULT   No I almost I (stammers) I didn't even get the chance to turn it and he grabbed.

CLARK   Okay when you say grabbed you, how?

TETREAULT   That I I think he he grabbed me like

CLARK   Like a bear hug?

TETREAULT   yeah like

CLARK   Type thing.

TETREAULT   a bear hug but then he had that Taser and he was tazering me on

CLARK   On the front?

TETREAULT   front.

CLARK   From behind, he's reaching around.

TETREAULT   Yeah yeah like like tazering me.

CLARK   Okay.

TETREAULT   And I'm going what's uh gain' on like cuz I'm thinking I don't know I'm thinking maybe this girl is playing a joke on me and and just trying to scare me.

CLARK   Right, was he hurting you at that time?

TETREAULT   No

CLARK   Like was it a

TETREAULT   But

CLARK   a strong bear hug?

TETREAULT   it was a strong bear hug but

CLARK   Mm hm.

TETREAULT   but the Taser uh for some reason well it did, wasn't hurting me. To me it wasn't hurting me. And I'm like what's gain' on at first I'm kinda off and I'm like what's what and then he we're struggling and then finally that's when I kinda turned back and then I see his face and then like a chill ran down my back cuz I seen him in a

CLARK   Okay

TETREAULT   mask you know.

CLARK   describe the mask.

TETREAULT   Urn see this the the thing I I (stammers) I see it now and then that that's the mask but at the time I I just remember thinking it's this hockey mask and it has the straps, and uh and it's painted up. That's all I remember.

CLARK   But you seen the mask on the media release yesterday.

TETREAULT   And then I then I like you know what that that

CLARK   When did you see

TETREAULT   that

CLARK   the mask?
TETREAULT   I (stammers)
CLARK   Like on the media thing. When did
you   see   that? Today's   Monday.   TETREAULT
      Yesterday.
CLARK   Yesterday on
TETREAULT   Yeah.
CLARK   TV?
TETREAULT   Yeah.
CLARK   What channel were you watching?
TETREAULT   Uh no I was saw it on the internet uh
my buddy
CLARK   Okay.
TETREAULT   uh sent me a CTV news article and it
had a video.   That's when I saw and then like okay yeah
know what it, that's probably the mask and I remember I
forgot to tell you in my story while we were struggling and
at that time when he's kinda punching me, I really wasn't
scared of him at this point cuz I uh I knew he didn't have
anything to hurt me, he didn't have the gun, the Taser so, I
actually grabbed his mask and I (stammers) pushed up on it
cuz I kinda wanted to take it off. I couldn't get it off, but I
could see part of his face. Urn and then urn he would now
that I see the guy that's him, that's the same build same
same
CLARK   Same build (overtalk)
TETREAULT   sort of (overtalk)
CLARK   but you didn't see his face (overtalk)
TETREAULT   (Unintelligible) face no (overtalk)
CLARK   so you wouldn't be (overtalk)
TETREAULT   not the whole (overtalk)
CLARK   able to say (overtalk)
TETREAULT   (Unintelligible) (overtalk)

CLARK   other than seeing it on the news.
TETREAULT   That's right.
CLARK   Pretty fair.
TETREAULT   That's right.
CLARK   But the mask (overtalk)
TETREAULT   That's why I say (overtalk)
CLARK   when when you saw the mask you're
saying that's the mask I saw.
TETREAULT   Yeah. I yeah.
CLARK   Okay. Okay. Okay I want you to I
know what's I need you to take me through the actual
struggle. Very slowly.
TETREAULT   That
CLARK   Yeah.
TETREAULT   I see I can't remember the whole
details
CLARK   Your best as you
TETREAULT   but I'll try.
CLARK   can. Like you, you're in a bear hug.
TETREAULT   Yeah.
CLARK   And he's sticking you with that.
TETREAULT   Yeah.
CLARK   And you (overtalk)
TETREAULT   And then uh we kinda
CLARK   you turn
TETREAULT   went all around
CLARK   like
TETREAULT   the garage. Like urn
CLARK   The whole garage like
TETREAULT   Not gar-
CLARK   is any part of it blocked off or is it
just you can go in the whole garage?
TETREAULT   Pretty much it was empty.

CLARK	Any tarps up anything like that?
TETREAULT	No.
CLARK	Nothing. Okay.
TETREAULT	No it was empty pretty empty.
CLARK	How dark
TETREAULT	It was (overtalk)
CLARK	like can you see one wall to the other

wall?

TETREAULT	Yes. Because there was (overtalk)
CLARK	Right when you walked in? Or did

your eyes have to take time to get used to that?

TETREAULT   Urn... maybe getting used to it just a slight bit uh it just because the door was part way open and it was seven o'clock at night and at that time there was still it was pretty light out still. I was able to, I was able to see the walls and see the door. But urn I don't know how I didn't see him. Like he must've been hiding behind the (stammers) by the door back there it must've been some kind of I can't remember if was some kinda little wall there in the corner.

CLARK	Okay.
TETREAULT	He must've been there I don't know.
CLARK	The first time you hear or see him is

when?

TETREAULT	When he grabbed me.
CLARK	Grab me so you don't hear him come

up behind you?

TETREAULT	No.
CLARK	Okay. Alright so this struggle is are

you still in a bear hug when you first started to struggle?

TETREAULT   Yes. Um he bear hugged me cuz he's tazering me and we go around urn (stammers) from the door to the um almost like the corner all the way to the not there's still a fair way maybe maybe half way to the middle of the garage. And that's when I stop kinda (stammers) struggling and I look back and that's when I seen the mask. So then urn that's when I turn around and I grab that Taser thing and I I put it down so I (stammers) to basically tell this guy this things not hurting me, quit, quit it, like uh like basically I'm saying what the hell is this, is this a joke, cuz you're not hurting me.

CLARK   So when you grab the Taser thing has he still got you in a bear hug?

TETREAULT   No

CLARK   Okay.

TETREAULT   not at this point.

CLARK   Which are you facing each other?

TETREAULT   Yes now I'm facing him.

CLARK   How far away?

TETREAULT   Uh barely... fairly close.

CLARK   Like closer than me and you?

TETREAULT   Oh yeah yeah. Yeah like (overtalk) urn. Like I had to be cuz I was holding the Taser from his hand right.

CLARK   So you're just

TETREAULT   He he didn't have it exit was just a small

CLARK   Right.

TETREAULT   and so I grabbed it. And I just like this and he kept triggering it so I'm fairly close to him at this point.

CLARK   Okay. And what does he do (stammers) how do you get that

TETREAULT   Oh he just

CLARK   away from him?

177

TETREAULT   stood there and I'm lookin' at him like you're not hurting me, quit quit doing this. What the hell is gain' on? And urn he (stammers) kept triggering, triggering it for a a few more times and then uh and then then (stammers) then I don't remember what happened. I know I remember letting go and I don't why maybe he took it back and put it away. That's the only thing I can think of because that's when or somehow and this is I don't remember it but we ended up urn closer towards the door now again and then that's when (overtalk)

CLARK   Okay which door?

TETREAULT   The the (overtalk)

CLARK   Overhead door?

TETREAULT   No the other door.

CLARK   The pedestrian door.

TETREAULT   Pedestrian door.

CLARK   The one that's closed.

TETREAULT   Right. For some reason and then that's when he pulled the gun out. And that's when I was closer to that door when he told me to go down on the floor.

CLARK   Okay.

TETREAULT   It was further.

CLARK   During the time of the bear hug

TETREAULT   Yeah.

CLARK   and the grab and the Taser.

TETREAULT   Yeah.

CLARK   Is there any other physical thing he's doing to you? Any punches thrown?

TETREAULT   No.

CLARK   Kicks?

TETREAULT   No.

CLARK   Not anything like that?

TETREAULT   Oh I forgot (stammers) not not at that time no but
CLARK   Okay. No and we'll get to all
TETREAULT   Okay okay.
CLARK   that stuff yeah. Cuz I know I just wanna refresh your memory
TETREAULT   Yeah I know (overtalk)
CLARK   no it's tough
TETREAULT   I'm starting to remember stuff
CLARK   Yeah you will and you will and that's normal that uh you know what I appreciate it cuz you're reliving it and you're just being honest.
TETREAULT   Yeah.
CLARK   And that's all I can ask right?
TETREAULT   Yeah.
CLARK   So and that's why I'm trying to just jog your memory
TETREAULT   Yeah.
CLARK   with those things.
TETREAULT   It it helps.
CLARK   It's what we do. So you're now at the point that you're back by the pedestrian door with him
TETREAULT   Yeah.
CLARK   very close to you?
TETREAULT   No there's now I'm a little further away for some reason. And but then he pulled like and this is I'm thinkin' hey I have enough uh time now to get away. But then he pulled the gun out. And then I'm like, I'm screwed now. I don't know if that guns real. I can't run, what if it is real I'm dead. And then I thought I was dead I I swear (stammers) like when they say your life flashed before your eyes (stammers) I I it almost as my family is going through my head I was like I'm never gonna see them

again, you know, stuff like this this and and uh basically once he pulled the gun out I was done I'm like okay, I'll just do what he wants.

CLARK   What does he say.

TETREAULT   He said urn get down on the ground, put your face toward the the floor or the cement and put your hands behind your back.

CLARK   Okay and what's

TETREAULT   So I'm like okay.

CLARK   how's he holding the gun?

TETREAULT   More

CLARK   Do you remember?

TETREAULT   closer to his, his side.

CLARK   Right hand then?

TETREAULT   Right hand, he's right handed. Did the

CLARK   Yeah.

TETREAULT   Taser in his right hand too.

CLARK   Alright. Urn so you go down on the ground.

TETREAULT   I did what he asked yup.

CLARK   Put your hands (overtalk)

TETREAULT   And I

CLARK   behind your back.

TETREAULT   Yeah and put my face down. Urn

CLARK   What does he do?

TETREAULT   He then urn uh cuz I can't see him like he's telling me put my head down and close my eyes as well. And I kinda kept peeking anyway and that's why I saw him pull the duct tape out. I don't know where he had the duct tape.

CLARK   Okay now where does he pull the duct tape out?

TETREAULT   I couldn't see cuz I couldn't see I didn't see the whole character.

CLARK   But you say pull it out so you're

TETREAULT   I (unintelligible) (overtalk)

CLARK   saying it's on his person?

TETREAULT   I have I think so.

CLARK   Okay.

TETREAULT   Yeah.

CLARK   Tell me what's

TETREAULT   Must have been.

CLARK   what does this guy Look like?

TETREAULT   Urn...

CLARK   Height, weight, that type of thing.

TETREAULT   Well see this is what I when when I told my friends I said he's he's way taller than me, he's probably like five ten. Bigger build than me. Urn (stammers) way stronger than me. That's all I could tell (stammers) I thought when I pulled the mask up, like couldn't get a good it was dark but (stammers) I pulled the mask I thought I saw freckles for some reason. And and I thought it was dark though and I thought um hey kinda thought reddish freckles but it could've been the mask rubbing on his face right. But uh I though oh God he has freckles so he must be your kinda you know (stammers) most people with red hair have red freckles.

CLARK   Yeah.

TETREAULT   That's what I thought in my head. This guy's probably red (Stammers) urn redhead I didn't see his hair though. And I just thought he probably has red hair and my first thought about twenty-two years old. He kinda looked younger like a punk I thought oh what a punk trying to

CLARK   Okay.

TETREAULT   mug me right. I thought it was a
whole mugging too.
CLARK   What is he wearing, other than the
mask?
TETREAULT   He's wearing a a kind of a brown
bunny-hug. Uh
CLARK   What do you mean a brown bunny-
hug.
TETREAULT   Bb- bunny-hu what your hoody.
CLARK   Oh hoody.
TETREAULT   He had a
CLARK   Yeah.
TETREAULT   hoody with the mask on.
CLARK   What color brown?
TETREAULT   Uh... I can't even it could've been uh
green too I guess but it no I'm I'm fairly sure it was kind' ve
a lighter brown.
CLARK   Lighter brown.
TETREAULT   Yeah.
CLARK   Okay. And did you notice what type
of pants or shoes?
TETREAULT   (Sighs) I think the shoes were kinda
uh kinda like boots. Uh cuz I don't remember thinking he
had runners on or anything he had kinda kinda like boot, he
had boots on. The pants I don't remember. I can't remember
if it was jeans or I don't I don't think I don't remember
thinking it was jeans. It was somethin' else.
CLARK   Okay.
TETREAULT   Yeah.
CLARK   Alright now you notice any facial
hair?
TETREAULT   None.
CLARK   None.

TETREAULT	He didn't have any.
CLARK	And what about nationality?
TETREAULT	He was white.
CLARK	White guy.
TETREAULT	Definitely. Yes. I know for--
CLARK	Okay. Now... you're down on the ground.
TETREAULT	Yeah.
CLARK	You've put your hands behind your back and you're trying to sneak a peek. You see him pull out the duct tape
TETREAULT	Yeah.
CLARK	what does he do?
TETREAULT (overtalk)	He cuts a piece but I don't know
CLARK	How
TETREAULT	how (overtalk)
CLARK	do you remember how?
TETREAULT	he cut it.
CLARK	Okay.
TETREAULT	I don't cuz I I had to go down urn... yeah I don't know. Yeah how he cut the tape. 1... and so then uh he just it was about this big maybe just enough to put over my eyes. Then that's what he did he put it over my eyes.
CLARK	And how does he do that? While you're laying on ground?
TETREAULT	Yeah.
CLARK	Do you lift, told you to lift your head up or what does he do?
TETREAULT	Yeah, I lifted it up to see, try to get a glimpse (stammers)

CLARK   And how is he standing there in relation to you then?

TETREAULT   Welll'm

CLARK   Like in front of you

TETREAULT   down on the ground

CLARK   beside you

TETREAULT   laying down and he's in front of me. And he kinda just leaned over and kinda just uh put the tape on my eyes.

CLARK   Do you know where the gun was at that time?

TETREAULT   No.

CLARK   Okay.

TETREAULT   I'm guessing he he (stammers) somehow he he was able to pull that out whenever he wanted to. Just he had it on him.

CLARK   Okay so after the duct tape what happens next?

TETREAULT   That's when urn... he went around me. And that's when he was gonna I thought he was gonna tie my hands up. Later I find out he's gonna handcuff me. But at the time I thought he was gonna tie, duct tape my hands or something. That's when I triggered me I'm like this is no standard robbery like... taping a guys eyes like he could'a taken my wallet, could'a taken my keys, my cell phone, anytime he wanted, I told him right at there while I'm laying down on the ground, I'll give you anything you want just let me go. He he responds yeah don't worry if you cooperate it'll just be a standard robbery. (Overtalk)

CLARK   Okay do you remember do you remember what he exactly said, his exact words?

TETREAULT   (Stammers) I don't remember his (stammers) exact words.

CLARK   Alright.
TETREAULT   But that was basically what he said.
CLARK   Okay.
TETREAULT   This will be a standard robbery like something like that.
CLARK   Alright. Are you doing any more talking to him while you're on the ground?
TETREAULT   (Sighs) no. I don't think ss•no because I'm thinking in my head what I'm going to be do. And urn that's at that point and I heard, I (stammers) couldn't see anymore. Just heard belt jiggling. Didn't know what he was doing, now that I think about it he was probably just taking his (stammers) his handcuffs off of his his belt. But at the time I didn't know, that's when I thought hey maybe he's pulling his pants down or something and I'm gonna get raped. I don't know. Urn but a lot of stuffs goin' through my head I (stammers) I didn't know if it was that I (stammers) I thought maybe he he's takin' somethin' else out to kill me with I don't know I there's a lot of stuffs goin' through my head so that's at this point for some reason I'm thinkin' of my family, my (stammers) everything... gain' through my head and I'm like I gotta take the chance I can't die like this. And that's when I he didn't he didn't handcuff me at that point yet so I ripped off the tape and got up and I yelled at him I
said I can't do this anymore. I can't no I can't, urn... I can't, I can't remember what I said now. Urn...
CLARK   That's fine (overtalk)
TETREAULT   I can't go down like this. I can't go down like this.
CLARK   Okay.
TETREAULT   I yelled at him. And he got mad.

CLARK   Okay what does he say to that reply
do you remember what he said? TETREAULT   Oh
then he (stammers) yelling at me to get back down on the
ground. He was very unhappy. That I got up. He kept
yelling get back down on the ground. Get back down on the
ground. And uh I don't think I responded to him (stammers)
but in but in my head it was like yeah right. (Unintelligible)
do this kind of thing and then that's when he pulled the gun
out again. Cuz he thought it would work again. Just like the
the first time when he pulled the gun out I did what he
asked, but not this time. I decided no I gotta take my
chances and at this time I'm more closer to him with the gun
in his hand. So now I get a better Look at the gun as weLL.
And I'm like I'm gonna take my chance. Like I said maybe a
BB gun, maybe a pellet gun whatever.

CLARK   And what's your position at this time
when you

TETREAULT   Now

CLARK   you stand up where are you and
where is he?

TETREAULT   (Stammers) (overtalk)

CLARK   Like if that's (overtalk)

TETREAULT   that's the (overtalk)

CLARK   (Unintelligible)

TETREAULT   (Unintelligible)

CLARK   use that as the pedestrian

TETREAULT   that's the door

CLARK   door.

TETREAULT   then now because I was laying here
and he was there when I was down on the ground, he came
around, that's when I got up and I said I I I took the tape off
and I said I can't do this and I turn around and now he's
standing there and I'm standing here closer to the door.

CLARK (unintelligible)   And   the   pedestrian   door

TETREAULT   Right.

CLARK   so you're up near that end

TETREAULT   Right.

CLARK   of the garage.

TETREAULT   And then um then what happens, so then that's when and he grabbed he must've grabbed me and um we started struggling. Oh and I'm guessing during this that's when I'm like okay I gotta try to fight. And that's something I missed actually, I tried punching him too but I was so weak. And I'm I'm like I remember I'm trying to punch him and I know I can't hit his mask cuz that's gonna hurt my hand so I'm trying to punch him in his chest. And I'm thinking man why am I so weak and my punches aren't... I feel like I'm not doing anything and it's like my punches are so weak. And then uh so I realize okay (Stammers) punching him not gonna do anything he's way bigger than me and I I'm not can't do anything so then I started I trying to kick him in the balls, and then uh he he after I started doing that he starts trying to do it to me too and I'm like jeez that's a little cheap you're the one mugging me why are you kicking me in the balls but whatever. So I was like

CLARK   Yeah.

TETREAULT   yeah. But I tried a few times doing that but...

CLARK   Did you get him?

TETREAULT   No.

CLARK   Did you hit him?

TETREAULT   No. Couldn't.

CLARK   And did he hit you?

TETREAULT   No.

CLARK   What about kick you?
TETREAULT   Uh he tried but he he I I swerved as
well. So I
CLARK   Like is this
TETREAULT   (Unintelligible) pretty good
CLARK   an all out intense battle
TETREAULT   shape too.
CLARK   or is it like
TETREAULT   No that's the thing is like this is the
whole thing this is what I'm thinking. While I'm doing this
this guy he had if he was more professional he could'a
(Stammers) killed me right away. Like right when I walked
in I didn't see him he could'a hit me over the head with a a
a bat, a baton or anything.
CLARK   Yeah.
TETREAULT   And could'a knocked me unconscious
right away. And I I don't know why he did that. His whole
plan was... to use this Taser thing on me first and that was
stupid on his part. But he had many chances to kill me, he
never did. So he had a that's why I thought afterward all this
happened he had a bigger plan for me I thought he maybe
he was gonna (stammers) handcuff me and take me
somewhere and do somethin'.
CLARK   Okay. So you're now...trying to
punch him you feel weak you're TETREAULT
        Yeah.
CLARK   trying to kick him you're not
connecting
TETREAULT   Yeah that's when he goes well since
you're not cooperating this is the way it has to be now. And
then then he starts punching me in my left side of my face.
And for some reason again... it would've been more
effective for him to punch me in the nose, the eyes, you

know something to cuz if he would've punched me (Stammers) I'd of been down right. But he's punching the side of the head trying to get my temple or knock me unconscious for some reason, I'm not sure but... it didn't work.

CLARK   Alright and where are you in relation to the door now

TETREAULT   (Unintelligible) (overtalk)

CLARK   (Unintelligible)

TETREAULT   but this is kind of we shuffled over now so I was facing him there with the gun.

CLARK   Now first of all you have a struggle with the gun though.

TETREAULT   Oh yeah that's right.

CLARK   Just before the punches.

TETREAULT   Yes that's before the punches, sorry.

CLARK   Okay tell me about the struggle with the gun.

TETREAULT   See now this is for, this is weird because I I'm facing this way, he pulls the gun out again. And for some I think cuz I I grab the gun somehow we maneuver we were urn struggling again, and I'm trying to break the gun right so we're struggling and somehow I ended up this way again. Struggling with this gun. And he's here back by the door okay. So because I just remember the door being there. And then I'm just trying (stammers) break this gun cuz this is (Laughs) I know it's plastic and I know if (stammers).

CLARK   What's he doing?

TETREAULT   He he's yelling at me cuz he doesn't want me touching his gun. And so then uh I wouldn't let go obviously but and I had a hold of his ar- his other arm just in case he tries to punch me in the (stammers) but he never did. And so we're just struggling I I'm just (stammers) you could tell it's just weird that cuz he if he was a real gun he would've fired it or whatnot, he never did, he had nothing and he didn't... he he never...just wasn't professional it was just like it was maybe his first time that's how I thought of it. And then and um I he was kind of letting me he do whatever I wanted to the gun he just he couldn't do anything cuz I had a good hold on it and I was just trying to break it and that's it he was just yelling at me yelling at me. Then I figure okay the guns fake whatever, but that's all I have right now. Then I look down I see the handcuffs. And then so I'm thinking uh the guns that's when I freaked out cuz I'm like oh my God this is way bigger than a mugging. Well I fly off the handle and I let go of the gun cuz I don't care about that anymore and I grab his handcuffs and he was mad again. I put the handcuffs around my fist cuz I was gonna punch try to punch him but then he just got madder and madder and kept telling me to put the handcuffs down on the ground down on the ground. I decided uh not worth getting him more mad... just decide to I might as well fight him for some reason I don't know why and so then I and he wanted me to put 'em down on the ground right in front of me I decided no I'm gonna throw 'em in the corner here. I threw it in in the corner. Um... then at this point... it's all I had basically it somehow now... he that's then grab each other still kinda just kinda wrestling but not really you know he just kinda good hold on me and and wrestling and I can't get away and then somehow we shifted all the way to over closer to the door.

CLARK   Mm hm.

TETREAULT   And but I'm this way now. Somehow we all shifted. And so then that's when he's uh I try kicking him in the balls um um that's when he head- bunted me.

Um then he starts trying to punch me in the face. But then I figure, hey I'm good nice close to the door let him punch me a few times and if I can move this way... and and which which worked, I'm closer to that door. And I know I can slip out of this jacket and just go run under the door. And so that's exactly what I did. I let him punch me a few times, maneuvering myself this way. And I knew he had a good hold of my jacket, I said perfect time, boom slipped out of the jacket. Slid under the door... pretty much. But then I once I got out I tried getting up and couldn't get up I couldn't run... I just felt so weak. And I just urn collapsed by my truck at the end of the truck. And um tried getting back up and he came right back after me.

CLARK   Which side of the truck are you on?

TETREAULT   Oh passenger side. Left side.

CLARK   Passenger side.

TETREAULT   Yeah.

CLARK   Okay.

TETREAULT   And so then urn I'm thinkin' okay I can't get up so that's when I try to grab this rock and then at the same time he grabs me, he must've grabbed me, I don't know how he grabbed me actually he's probably by my... (Unintelligible) waist or my my legs or something and drags me back.

CLARK   While you're on the ground he's pulling you back in.

TETREAULT   Yeah. And that's when I (overtalk) (unintelligible)

CLARK   Does he say anything

TETREAULT   that rock.

CLARK   at that time?

TETREAULT   No.

CLARK   Are you saying anything at that time?

191

TETREAULT   No.

CLARK   Okay.

TETREAULT   And he drags me back and I we both somehow he got me mostly under the garage... and then he went to go underneath and that's and I'm thinkin' in my head oh my God I have no other way to get away from this guy if I can't get away now. And for some reason, I don't remember anything but (stammers) some reason he must've let me go to get under the garage and that's when I decide I gotta go again. Try it. Got back under outside.

CLARK   So you were already, you were pulled right back into the garage fully?

TETREAULT   Fully uh but I was right by the the door right it was open whatever.

CLARK   Right.

TETREAULT   Waist high and then I can I can still I'm I'm laying on the ground though and then so I can still crawl underneath the door fair very easily.

CLARK   Right.

TETREAULT   And he... I think he had stood he had to get under and he had stood up, and then that's when I went back. For some reason, urn that's when uh he didn't come after me right away. And that's when I start running. And this time I was able to run better. And I was that's when I got to the walking path. And my whole plan when I got there was I knew there was a street up in front I was gonna stop a car, go to a house, anything I could to get away from this guy (unintelligible) I didn't know if I it would succeed cuz I was so weak. But it just so happened that that couple was there. And then uh... it just so happened that the couple was there and then for some reason like I said it took a little bit for him to come so my best guess is that he went to get his handcuffs but I don't

know if that's true or not. I don't know. So then uh uh (sighs) that's when I talk to the couple I was so exhausted I just kinda leaned over and I I don't know.

CLARK   Okay so where where exactly are they now in relation to the (Stammers) garage cuz you, you know when you come out of the garage

TETREAULT   Come out of the garage there's the back alley

CLARK   Which way did you go?

TETREAULT   Uh to the left.

CLARK   Okay.

TETREAULT   There was a walking path right

CLARK   Right.

TETREAULT   Goes

CLARK   Which way on the walking path?

TETREAULT   Uh is the couple?

CLARK   Yeah which way do you go?

TETREAULT   Um I actually went uh pretty straight. Uh from the back alley because the couple was to my left. But I was gonna go left. That was my whole plan.

CLARK   So you were going to go out to the main street.

TETREAULT   Yes.

CLARK   Which would be Fortieth Avenue.

TETREAULT   That's right, that's right. That's my whole (overtalk)

CLARK   Okay.

TETREAULT   plan, that's what I was gonna (overtalk)

CLARK   Yeah.

TETREAULT   do just because (overtalk)

CLARK   They're right

TETREAULT   more traffic (overtalk)

CLARK	more beside the garage then?
TETREAULT	They were right there.
CLARK	On the walking path.
TETREAULT	Yeah.
CLARK	Okay.
TETREAULT	To my left.

CLARK   So so they know which garage you come from or not?

TETREAULT	I have no idea.
CLARK	Okay.

TETREAULT   I just kinda pointed I said uh uh I doubt it I don't think they knew.

CLARK   Okay.

TETREAULT   Actually. And so because they wouldn't of saw me come out.

CLARK	They just see you on the path.
TETREAULT	Right.
CLARK	Come outta nowhere.
TETREAULT	That's right.
CLARK	Okay.

TETREAULT   So then uh they're a Little shocked and I I'm saying I I'm in my head I'm thinkin' oh thank God there's people. Oh by the way... while I'm with this couple there's this jogger that comes through. And uh tall guy I don't know I didn't bother stopping him it was just, he was on a mission and he was

CLARK	Yeah.
TETREAULT	going yeah so but uh
CLARK	Okay.

TETREAULT   I decide I'll just talk to these people they're just staying here.

CLARK	Well the couple has come forward.
TETREAULT	Oh great.

CLARK   So we have identified them.
TETREAULT   Great.
CLARK   So that's good.
TETREAULT   Yeah I was hoping I didn't know if they were gonna help me or call or whatnot but yeah. Urn... so then urn... yeah that's when I said hey guy I think something like (Stammers) being mugged or attacked. Urn he's after me please help me, help me or something like that.
CLARK   What did they say to you?
TETREAULT   Nothing.
CLARK   Nothing.
TETREAULT   Nothing, they just stood there in shock. Just wow. Yeah with their dog.
CLARK   Yeah.
TETREAULT   And uh that I remember, I don't remember them saying anything they just stood there. And then the guy came after me right. And then they're like holy shit, there's a guy in a mask. I might'a said he had a mask on, I don't remember though, I don't think so. But...
CLARK   But so the guy comes right up to the walking path where
TETREAULT   Almost.
CLARK   you guys are?
TETREAULT   Almost.
CLARK   Like where how close?
TETREAULT   Cuz he was his mission uh... I'm on the walking path so he didn't actually get to the walking path and then urn I yelled that's the guy cuz I just, the couples right close to me. So then uh like the couple look and he's coming out and he looks and he's like holy sh- kinda probably holy crap right. Because then he he's like oh people oh oh and I have my mask on. Oh that looks a little

weird right. And that's what I figure would happen. So then uh he pretended he was my best friend or something and he kinda pretended like he was gonna lift the mask up or something and he turned around right away.

CLARK   And what when you say pretended like best friend can you remember what he said there?

TETREAULT   I can't remember. Somethin' like uh... hey Fred or... or (stammers) hey friend and I'm thinkin' (stammers) yeah nice you know I couldn't really talk much.

CLARK   Okay. So how long is that couple there? Like how long is that period of time?

TETREAULT   Not very long. That that didn't take very long. Urn... that whole time maybe a minute or two maybe.

CLARK   How long does the guy in the mask stay out there?

TETREAULT   Not very long as soon as he saw the people he went back.

CLARK   Oh did he?

TETREAULT   Yeah.

CLARK   And do you watch him go right back?

TETREAULT   I watched yeah I watched him for a bit and then I'm... then I knew I
needed to talk to this couple. Help me, help help.

CLARK   But when you watch him for a bit where at what point do you lose sight of him?

TETREAULT   Probably urn... when he got to my truck.

CLARK   Was he in the driveway?

TETREAULT   Yeah.

CLARK	Would the couple see where he went?
TETREAULT	Maybe. I don't know.
CLARK	Like like would the couple not know he went into the garage?
TETREAULT	I don't know.
CLARK	Did you see him go in the garage?
TETREAULT	No.
CLARK	Okay.
TETREAULT	But I knew he was going back there.
CLARK	Okay. So you know he's going back to the garage, he's in the area of the garage. What do you do next?
TETREAULT	That's when I um that's when the couple kept going. And um... they pass me... and I (stammers) basically uh yelled out to 'em and I said (stammers) aren't you gonna help me out. I couldn't believe they weren't going to help me, cuz I I just struggled with this guy
CLARK	Right.
TETREAULT	twenty-five thirty minutes. Whatever so then uh... (unintelligible) I said uh aren't you going to help me out well and he he felt bad, he he wanted to help. And he (Stammers) started coming back. And uh... he then um, but his girlfriend called him and then he went back to her.
CLARK	And where are they now?
TETREAULT	Now they're passed me on the walking path going north.
CLARK	Going north so
TETREAULT	Yeah.
CLARK	away from Fortieth Avenue.
TETREAULT	Right.

197

CLARK	Okay.
TETREAULT	So
CLARK	Are you in the alley now?
TETREAULT	I'm still in the same spot.
CLARK	Or in the or on on the walking path?
TETREAULT	walking path.

CLARK   But you're on the nor•on the south side of the alley?

TETREAULT	Uh no
CLARK	And they're on the north side
TETREAULT	I'm in the middle, right in the middle

of the back

CLARK   Of the alley. And the walking path (stammers) cuz the walking path

TETREAULT   Cut's right through.

CLARK   crosses the alley but the path actually stops right cuz the alley runs in-between 'im.

TETREAULT   Yeah there's uh I'm still on the cement of the the walking path so.

CLARK	Okay.
TETREAULT	Uh yeah.
CLARK	Alright..

TETREAULT   Urn... so then uh oh then I call out again uh can't you help me out just ta watch me get to my truck. And uh he starts coming back again and and his girlfriend calls him back. And so uh I said fine I'll just do it myself because I knew at this point, whatever... urn I didn't even think uh (stammers) I was too absentminded I wasn't thinking proper but I could'a called the cops at that point but I didn't even think I was just stay alive somehow. So then uh I thought okay I can do a few things I could follow them which, that's gonna freak •em out even more. Or I could go toward the street, the Fortieth Ave street. Like my my original plan was to stop a car, go to a house, or something. Urn but then I thought you know what... I have the advantage at this point I he thinks I'm the couples still there, or still talking to me. He's not gonna come out for a bit. So uh I'm gonna try going back to my truck, then Locking the doors, and then even if he comes out and uh he has to break the windows to get to me, and it's much safer. Then I can

CLARK   Right.

TETREAULT   turn the truck on and leave there right. So that's what I did and I started, I locked, I started the truck.   I I that when I came back I saw, he was in the garage I saw his feet pacing back and forth. My jacket on the ground, in the garage. And then I urn... I got in my truck, started it, he didn't even come out um I drove, backed up, drove out, looked at the door, he stayed in the garage.

CLARK   In a hurry or?

TETREAULT   I drove out in a hurry yeah.

CLARK   Did you get the address when you left or?

TETREAULT   No.

CLARK   Okay.

TETREAULT   I still didn't know the address till I uh people (stammers) till yesterday.

CLARK   Till you saw it on the news?

TETREAULT   I just knew it was Fortieth Ave, I knew the directions, I knew the garage.

CLARK   Right.

TETREAULT   But I didn't know the actual house number.

CLARK   Okay. Um... through this here... was the garage door ever closed? TETREAULT No.

CLARK   Even when you were driving away it
still remained open?
TETREAULT   Right.
CLARK   Okay. You had mentioned that you
were thinking uh time wise (overtalk)
TETREAULT   Yeah (overtalk)
CLARK   (Stammers) but (overtalk)
TETREAULT   to me it felt (overtalk)
CLARK   the whole incident from the time you
first got into the garage to the time you got your truck, how
long was that?
TETREAULT   It felt like thirty minutes.
CLARK   That long eh? How long do you think
you and I have been talking right now?
TETREAULT   Probably at least thirty or forty
minutes.
CLARK   Okay. Alright. Um cuz that that
struggle time and that is a long time.
TETREAULT   I know. And that's what I thought
CLARK   Yeah.
TETREAULT   why I was so weak.
CLARK   Yeah well when your adrenalines
fulluh (stammers) you know if you ever do you place sports
at all or anything llke that?
TETREAULT   Uh (stammers) a little bit but I
haven't played (overtalk)
CLARK   Ever been involved in a fight in
hockey?
TETREAULT   No.
CLARK   (Unintelligible) thirty seconds
TETREAULT   I don't play hockey.
CLARK   and you're wiped out. You know.
TETREAULT   Yeah yeah.

CLARK	I've had a few of those in my day.
TETREAULT	Got'cha.
CLARK	And it's like you're you're done.
TETREAULT	I know.
CLARK	Thirty forty seconds it's over.
TETREAULT	Yeah.
CLARK	It's it's quick

TETREAULT   Yeah. It it might of. It might of been quicker than that but it felt to me Like twenty

CLARK	Right.
TETREAULT	twenty-five thirty minutes that whole
CLARK	Do (overtalk)

TETREAULT   (Unintelligible)   probably   thirty minutes.

CLARK   Do you ever remember uh take your mind back do you ever remember looking do you have a clock in your truck for example? Do you remember looking at

TETREAULT	I do
CLARK	a time?
TETREAULT	(Sighs)

CLARK   When you're driving away, when you happen to park (overtalk) TETREAULT   Yeah because I thought

CLARK	on your way home?

TETREAULT   it was like seven forty-five when I was driving away.

CLARK	Why do you think that?
TETREAULT	I just remember looking at the clock
CLARK	Okay.
TETREAULT	and thinking it was seven forty-five.
CLARK	So and you (overtalk)

TETREAULT   It was (stammers) starting to get dark.

CLARK   And you were thinking you got there at what time?

TETREAULT   Seven fifteen.

CLARK   Do you remember looking at your clock when you got there?

TETREAULT   Yeah I look at my watch I thought I'm I'm alma- it wasn't quite seven fifteen uh cuz I was supposed to be

CLARK   Okay

TETREAULT   there at seven and I almost

CLARK   So then you're right

TETREAULT   fifteen minutes late

CLARK   you're right around thirty minute mark.

TETREAULT   Yeah.

CLARK   Okay. Now... you obviously had a thought that either you had mentioned that he was gonna kill you or rape you, that was going through your mind.

TETREAULT   Mm hm.

CLARK   Urn... do you do you was that your impression your got if if he would've got you restrained that that would happen to you?

TETREAULT   Yes.

CLARK   Okay.

TETREAULT   I thought he was gonna actually I thought he was not gonna do it there though I thought my impression was he was gonna do it somewhere he was gonna cuz I didn't know why he would handcuff me to leave me there to kill me. I thought he was gonna bring me to somewhere secluded and kill me.

CLARK   Okay and I guess at what point does it click in your mind this is a setup?

TETREAULT   (Laughs) right way

CLARK   Right away?

TETREAULT   after I got he he attacked me from behind.

CLARK   Right away eh?

TETREAULT   Like I've been setup.

CLARK   Gain' oh no.

TETREAULT   Yeah.

CLARK   Okay. Your jacket that was

TETREAULT   Yeah.

CLARK   left behind. Describe that to me.

TETREAULT   Black, has Old Navy written in the back and

CLARK   Old Navy?

TETREAULT   very thin. Yeah.

CLARK   Inside outside?

TETREAULT   Inside. Uh very thin kind of a summer jacket. Uh smaller cuz I'm a smaller kind of guy.

CLARK   What kind of pockets?

TETREAULT   Uh just the normal pockets on (stammers) each side. Uh...

CLARK   Did you have anything in it?

TETREAULT   I don't remember I I don't think so cuz I remember thinking the (Stammers) pockets suck cuz they're not deep enough so I try not to leave anything in the pockets.

CLARK   Good thing.

TETREAULT   Yeah that's what I thought because

CLARK   No keys.

TETREAULT   no I had my keys on me (unintelligible)

CLARK   No uh wallet.
TETREAULT   No I had my wallet on me in my
jeans.
CLARK   Good thing.
TETREAULT   That's the thing... when I was down
he could'a just taken my wallet.
Taken my cell phone, it was on my belt. Taken anything he
wanted I was I was letting him. CLARK   Did
you lose (overtalk)
TETREAULT   And he didn't (overtalk)
CLARK   any of that stuff?
TETREAULT   nothing.
CLARK   Nothing.
TETREAULT   The only thing I lost was my jacket.
CLARK   Oh.
TETREAULT   And I was very lucky.
CLARK   The pockets are they on the side on
the outside is it (overtalk)
TETREAULT   Yeah they're (overtalk)
CLARK   inside pocket (overtalk)
TETREAULT   on the outside (overtalk)
CLARK   and are they zipper or?
TETREAULT   No no zipper.
CLARK   And you said you saw that in there?
TETREAULT   Yeah I saw it on the ground when I
came back.
CLARK   In the garage or outside?
TETREAULT   In the middle of the garage yeah.
CLARK   Yeah but you could see it through the
under the door.
TETREAULT   I could see him pacing in the front
there.

CLARK   When he's pacing is the lights on in the garage now are they still off
TETREAULT   No.
CLARK   still off eh.
TETREAULT   Right.
CLARK   Okay. Alright just let me go check with my partner I just wanna make sure I've covered everything with you
TETREAULT   Alright.
CLARK   here. And I'll find out what's happening with the tech guys. And I might have a few
TETREAULT   Okay.
CLARK   more questions for you. Okay?
TETREAULT   Sure.
CLARK   Do you need uh anything right now?
TETREAULT   No.
CLARK   A pop or anything like
TETREAULT   I'm good.
CLARK   that? You're good?
TETREAULT   Yeah.
CLARK   Okay. (Door opens and closes)
Elapsed time 01:22:47
Elapsed time 01:37:54
CLARK   (Door opens) Okay just a couple things to cover and then uh
TETREAULT   Sure.
CLARK   (Door closes) we'll get'cha outta here.
TETREAULT   Alright.
CLARK   Do you remember anything about his voice?
TETREAULT   Very commanding.
CLARK   Okay.

TETREAULT   Like uh authoritative kinda... it's uh manly it's uh you know very

CLARK   Okay.

TETREAULT   like he wasn't joking around kind of thing.

CLARK   Any type of uh tone like uh not tone but uh accent anything different about it?

TETREAULT   No.

CLARK   No. Is it something you think you'll remember or?

TETREAULT   Yeah possibly.

CLARK   Okay. Urn... and again don't think I'm judging you

TETREAULT   Mm hm.

CLARK   cuz I'm not

TETREAULT   Yeah.

CLARK   but why did you not go to the police? What was your reasoning there?

TETREAULT   I don't know I was uh after it was all over it was like I was scared and I was uh maybe a little bit ashamed. I don't know.

CLARK   Okay.

TETREAULT   I don't, I don't uh

CLARK   When you talked to your friends did they (overtalk)

TETREAULT   They kept telling me to go and I didn't.

CLARK   Okay.

TETREAULT   It was that's my fault.

CLARK   Now don't you know what... uh we can't second guess

TETREAULT   Yeah.

CLARK   that you know it's just but it's a question I have to ask.

TETREAULT   For sure.

CLARK   Urn in regards to the profile you mentioned that you went on the computer a couple hours after (stammers) remember you laid down

TETREAULT   Yeah.

CLARK   at your place.

TETREAULT   Yeah.

CLARK   Was your profile gone too like how can

TETREAULT   No no no.

CLARK   your profile, your profiles there?

TETREAULT   My profile I have to physically take it off.

CLARK   Okay so yours is still there. When you're talkin' profiles erased it's the other one.

TETREAULT   Their uh their profile was gone. And

CLARK   The spider

TETREAULT   Spiderwebzz profile was gone.

CLARK   Spiderwebzz profile is gone.

TETREAULT   And uh (stammers) in this uh website you can actually delete your sent (stammers) and received messages yourself I guess and so they were all gone too.

CLARK   So

TETREAULT   Right on the website.

CLARK   okay.

TETREAULT   That's that's the only way we communicated.

CLARK   Alright.

TETREAULT   So I wasn't like (stammers) I was thinkin' and because I was going to go copy everything I talked to her about. Just in case I was gonna come in right. And--

CLARK   Did you ever

TETREAULT   It was all gone.

CLARK   get any emails after that? Any threats or anything like that?

TETREAULT   Nothing.

CLARK   Nothing eh?

TETREAULT   They're complete gone. I did uh remove my profile for a bit though. Cuz I was kinda scared and so I believe I took it off for a couple days so. Then I put it back on.

CLARK   Okay. Was there (stammers) ever any threats by him? Anything like that?

TETREAULT   What do you mean? Urn what kind of threats?

CLARK   Like uh any type of verbal threats about going to the police or anything like that

TETREAULT   No.

CLARK   anytime do you ever remember anything like that?

TETREAULT   No.

CLARK   Okay and what about um by you. Do you ever remember saying anything about not going to the police or

TETREAULT   I might of.

CLARK   if you (unintelligible)

TETREAULT   I said uh yeah I I when I was down on the ground, he had the gun I I might'a said (stammers) um just take what you want and just let me go and I can't remember if I said you know I won't go to I won't go to the cops or something. (Stammers) I might of but I can't remember for sure.

CLARK	Okay.
TETREAULT	Yeah.
CLARK	Alright.
TETREAULT	But uh (stammers) from what I think

I don't think I said that.

CLARK	Okay. Um what I was gonna do is

just grab the tech guys

TETREAULT	Okay.
CLARK	and they'll just drive up to your house

and if they can meet'cha there. TETREAULT   Sure.

CLARK	And they'll grab that computer now.

And then we'll have it and then they can get everything
back to you here.

TETREAULT	Yeah in a couple
CLARK	As quick as
TETREAULT	days or
CLARK	possible.
TETREAULT	what?
CLARK	Yeah.
TETREAULT	Days?
CLARK	They said it would it only take like a

day just

TETREAULT	Okay.
CLARK	they they can when they come to

your house you can ask 1em they can they'll know all that
stuff.

TETREAULT	Alright.
CLARK	And uh they're gonna explain to you

what they can do with that and what they're

TETREAULT	That's fine.
CLARK	gonna do and all that
TETREAULT	Yeah
CLARK	stuff.

TETREAULT   As long as I get it back that will be great.
CLARK   Oh yeah.
TETREAULT   (Laughs)
CLARK   I I I you'll have it back uh like I say I would think by Wednesday at the latest
TETREAULT   Okay.
CLARK   is the way they're telling me but they'll be able to fill you in more on that.
TETREAULT   Sure.
CLARK   And uh I'll just see if they here and then we'll get going. Are you parked out front?
TETREAULT   I'm parked in the across the street in that
CLARK   Okay.
TETREAULT   parking lot.
CLARK   I'll be right back.
TETREAULT   Sure. (Door opens and closes)
Elapsed time 01:41:58
Elapsed time 01:42:27
CLARK   (Door opens) Okay Gilles
TETREAULT   Okay.
CLARK   Uh they're actually here now

Recording ends

Transcribed by: Bobbie
Proofread by: Bobbie
2009 Sep 21

Det. B. CLARK REG# 1179
09/09

Appendix 3 - Detective Johnson Interview

TRANSCRIPT OF A KGB INTERVIEW
Between Detective Dale JOHNSON & Gilles
TETREAULT
On 2009 September 22
At Edmonton Police Services Headquarters

File #08-137180

(Background noise)
Elapsed time 00:00:53
(Door closes)
Elapsed time 00:04:02

JOHNSON	(Door opens) Just have a seat there.
TETREAULT	Sure.
JOHNSON	(Door closes) Same room different sofas then last time.
TETREAULT	Yeah yeah. I noticed that (laughs).
JOHNSON	You did eh? Yeah they're leather.
TETREAULT	Yeah nice.
JOHNSON	So so Gilles I wanna first off thank you for coming in.
TETREAULT	Okay.
JOHNSON	Uh my understanding is you were speaking to Jeff KERR.
TETREAULT	Yes.
JOHNSON	And uh Frank METSELAAR.
TETREAULT	Right. I didn't actually
JOHNSON	They're...
TETREAULT	get to talk to Frank but...
JOHNSON	No.

TETREAULT	he left me a message (laughs).
JOHNSON	Left you some messages.
TETREAULT	Yeah yeah.
JOHNSON	Uh well unfortunately they're both

not available today

TETREAULT	Yeah
JOHNSON	so they asked me to um sort of sub in

for them.

TETREAULT	Okay.
JOHNSON	But, I believe you know why you're

here.

TETREAULT	Yeah
JOHNSON	In essence
TETREAULT	Jeff told me last time I was
JOHNSON	okay in essence to review
TETREAULT	(Stammers)
JOHNSON	your previous statement.
TETREAULT	Yeah.
JOHNSON	I don't have to tell you the

importance of your uh uh your evidence. And

TETREAULT	right.
JOHNSON	the Prosecutor feels that uh he would

like you to review your statement.

TETREAULT	Mm hm.
JOHNSON	And basically swear to it.
TETREAULT	Okay.
JOHNSON	Uh to uh its truthfulness. So that's

what we're here to ex- (stammers) go through an exercise to
uh ensure that that's done.

TETREAULT	Okay.
JOHNSON	Uh we're I'd like to start I'm gonna

have to I'm gonna read through a form

TETREAULT	Mm hm.

JOHNSON   for you and you just (stammers) pay attention and then we'll uh (Stammers) on your on your uh choice.

TETREAULT   Mm hm.

JOHNSON   You can swear to it on the Bible.

TETREAULT   For sure.

JOHNSON   Or or if you're not a religious person we can uh solemnly affirm or solemnly declare.

TETREAULT   Mm hm.

JOHNSON   uh and then I have

TETREAULT   What's (overtalk)

JOHNSON   a TV set up here we'll I'll allow you in private to view your statement from uh I believe it was last November.

TETREAULT   It was uh yeah

JOHNSON   Right.

TETREAULT   beginning of November.

JOHNSON   I think it was so. I (stammers) my understanding is that interview is about (clears throat) say an hour an hour and a half

TETREAULT   Okay.

JOHNSON   Long.

TETREAULT   Yeah.

JOHNSON   So I'll leave you in here private, you can review your statement and uh during that time if you have any issues or uh you need to use a washroom or anything like that

TETREAULT   Mm hm.

JOHNSON   I'll just uh you can just knock on the door and I'll come and come and take care of whatever needs.

TETREAULT   Okay.

JOHNSON   Okay. So let me just uh go through this this form.

TETREAULT   Sure.

JOHNSON   Uh it has a title to it called a KGB Warning.

TETREAULT   Mm hm.

JOHNSON   That's uh of no concern to you it's just a title that was given, it relates to uh actually a Supreme Court of Canada ruling, uh doesn't mean

TETREAULT   (Laughs)

JOHNSON   Soviet Union

TETREAULT   Yeah that's

JOHNSON   KGB or

TETREAULT   what it sounds like.

JOHNSON   anything. I know it's just uh unfortunate coincidence I think.

TETREAULT   Yeah.

JOHNSON   But anyway. I'm going it says uh this statement will be taken by oath, solemn affirmation, or solemn declaration, and will be videotaped. You must understand that (stammers) that it is a criminal offence to mislead a police officer during a (stammers) an investigation. You may be liable to prosecution under section one forty of the Criminal Code of Canada if you mislead a police officer during this investigation and if convicted you could be sentenced to up to five years in jail.

TETREAULT   Mm hm.

JOHNSON   You must also understand that it is a criminal offence to attempt to obstruct justice during a police investigation, and if you do so you could be prosecuted under section one thirty-nine of the Criminal Code of Canada and if convicted be sentenced up to ten years in jail. You must further understand that you may be a witness at a trial concerning the events you describe in your statement. If at any time you change your statement or claim not to remember the events, the contents of the statement you now give may be used as evidence at the trial. In such circumstances you may be Liable to prosecution for fabricating evidence under section one thirty-seven of the Criminal Code of Canada, and if convicted you could be sentenced to up (stammers) up to fourteen years in jail. Do you understand the criminal consequences of making a false statement?

TETREAULT   I do.

JOHNSON   Okay. Alright it's uh twenty-second of

TETREAULT   Mm hm.

JOHNSON   September.

TETREAULT   Yeah.

JOHNSON   Gilles how do you uh spell your first name?

TETREAULT   G.I.L.L.E.S.

JOHNSON   Okay. Can you spell me your last name as well please?

TETREAULT   And the last name is T.E.T.R.E.A.U.L.T.

JOHNSON   Okay. I'm just gonna slide over here.

TETREAULT   Yeah.

JOHNSON   (Clears throat) Okay I'll have you uh sign there

TETREAULT   Mm hm.

JOHNSON   just acknowledging you uh received the above warning. Okay. And I'll do the same as a witness. Perfect. Okay now this the second part I spoke of.

TETREAULT   Okay.

JOHNSON	Uh now depending on your religious leanings.
TETREAULT	Yeah.
JOHNSON	Uh are you religious?
TETREAULT	I am yeah.
JOHNSON	Okay.
TETREAULT	The Bible's fine (overtalk)
JOHNSON	Okay Bible's fine.
TETREAULT	Yeah.
JOHNSON	Okay, you just can hold the Bible in your right hand.
TETREAULT	In my right hand.
JOHNSON	I'll just cross off here the solemn (stammers) affirmation
TETREAULT	Okay.
JOHNSON	we won't use it.
TETREAULT	Okay.
JOHNSON	Cross the solemn declaration we won't use it.
TETREAULT	Mm hm.
JOHNSON	And then I'll just Gilles.
TETREAULT	Okay.
JOHNSON	I forgot already. Two L's or one?
TETREAULT	Yes yeah one uh two L's.
JOHNSON	(Laughs)
TETREAULT	Yes.
JOHNSON	There we go.
TETREAULT	Yeah. R.E.
JOHNSON	Oh R.E.
TETREAULT	Yeah.
JOHNSON	A.U.
TETREAULT	L.T.

JOHNSON   L.T. Right. Okay. Do you Gilles
TETREAULT swear that the evidence you give as touching
the matters in question in this matter shall be the truth, the
whole truth, and nothing but the truth, so help you God?
TETREAULT   I do.
JOHNSON   Okay. Sworn in Edmonton. Twenty-
second day... September. Two thousand nine.
TETREAULT   Mm hm.
JOHNSON   And that's sign there please.
Excellent. I'm a Commissioner of Oaths, I'll sign this. Okay.
Thank you.
TETREAULT   No problem.
JOHNSON   That's through the formality part.
TETREAULT   Yeah.
JOHNSON   Alright. I'll uh just get a little
television set up here.
TETREAULT   Okay.
JOHNSON   There's a pad and a pen okay for your
convenience. Let's see here. Okay. Just got one of these
little portable DVD players here.
TETREAULT   Yeah. Handy.
JOHNSON   Gearing' up. Okay. Okay.
TETREAULT   Should I just sit over here?
JOHNSON   No I'm gonna
TETREAULT   Oh
JOHNSON   I'm gonna pull the table over just as
soon as I get things playing.
TETREAULT   Okay.
JOHNSON   And I believe the sound should be
adequate.
TETREAULT   Okay.
JOHNSON   If it's not I can put some earphones in
and you can listen through earphones but.

TETREAULT   Okay.

JOHNSON   Coming through the TV speakers I think it, I think it should be adequate.

TETREAULT   Sure.

JOHNSON   It's got some volume here. Okay. So do you want a water or pop or some

TETREAULT   Um

JOHNSON   snacks or anything? Are you fine?

TETREAULT   Um I'll actually maybe a glass of water (stammers).

JOHNSON   Okay. I'll uh run and get you some water. So is that playing?

TETREAULT   Yeah it...it's running.

JOHNSON   It's running.

TETREAULT   Yeah.

JOHNSON   Okay. Yeah and the volumes there I think the sound should be good.

TETREAULT   Okay yeah.

JOHNSON   And feel free to adjust it if you need to.

TETREAULT   It's all good.

JOHNSON   Okay, just a water (door opens) no snacks?

TETREAULT   Thank you. No I'm good.

JOHNSON   No I'll be right back. (door closes)

Elapsed time 00: 12:04

Previously recorded interview being viewed transcribed under separate document.

Elapsed time 00: 13:00

TETREAULT   (Door opens) thank you very much.

JOHNSON   Working fine?

TETREAULT   Yeah.

JOHNSON   Okay. If it's easier with the lights off—

TETREAULT   No it's good. (Door closes)

Elapsed time 00:13:08

Elapsed time 01:54:27

JOHNSON   (Door opens) Alright Gilles.

TETREAULT   Yeah.

JOHNSON   It's (door closes) that's it is it.

TETREAULT   That's it.

JOHNSON   Okay. Okay. Alright we appreciate you uh goin' through that.

TETREAULT   No problem.

JOHNSON   Okay I (stammers) only have uh two basic questions for you.

TETREAULT   Sure.

JOHNSON   And that would be uh is there anything that you would like add?

TETREAULT   Urn...

JOHNSON   (Unintelligible)

TETREAULT   Oh yeah when I when I was watching it I started remembering something well uh actually I thought of it last couple last couple months. When I walked in I remember thinking there's a shelving unit to the left. I'm pretty positive that there was some kind of shelving unit cuz I remember thinkin' I gotta if I'm struggling with this guy I can't I wanna stay away from that wall cuz there's some kind of I'm pretty sure some kind of shelving unit and I didn't wanna get myself hurt if I slammed into it.

JOHNSON   Okay.

TETREAULT   Um and also now that I think about it, in my interview I said I didn't know where he came out of. I'm pretty positive he's on the other side of the garage right so

JOHNSON   Okay.

TETREAULT   then he was just watching for me grab the door and then.

JOHNSON   Okay. This shelving unit you descri- or you talk about can you describe it at all?

TETREAULT   I think it was I I'm can't I think it's metal, metal shelving unit but I (stammers) I'm not positive.

JOHNSON   Okay.

TETREAULT   Yeah uh there was (stammers) a whole bunch of junk on it. (Stammers) pretty sure I can

JOHNSON   Okay.

TETREAULT   urn

JOHNSON   When you descri- when you say the word shelving unit to me that means uh

TETREAULT   Uh

JOHNSON   something against the wall.

TETREAULT   yeah.

JOHNSON   It's floor to ceiling or how tall is this, this thing you're describing?

TETREAULT   Oh man, I don't even remember, I just remember some kind of shelving unit. But it didn't go all the way to the wall uh all the way to the (stammers) the the top of the garage. No no.

JOHNSON   Okay. And you say you think?

TETREAULT   (Stammers)

JOHNSON   No continue go ahead.

TETREAULT   No I (stammers) I'm pretty positive there was something there.

JOHNSON   Okay fair enough.

TETREAULT   Um

JOHNSON   Okay.

TETREAULT   and what else, I think it's about it. When I (stammers) I miss some well I didn't say for some reason I didn't say it but when I got, first got out of the the um when I first got away and got outside of the garage I (stammers) I fell and then I start crawling.

JOHNSON   Okay.

TETREAULT   And for some reason I didn't tell him that.

JOHNSON   Okay.

TETREAULT   And that's when he grabbed me by the legs and he started dragging me back. And then that's when I tried to pick up the rock and it slipped out of my hand and then he threw me back into the garage.

JOHNSON   Okay. I understand.

TETREAULT   Yeah.

JOHNSON   Okay anything

TETREAULT   Um--

JOHNSON   else you'd like to add Gilles?

TETREAULT   I think it's about it.

JOHNSON   Okay.

TETREAULT   Covered everything mostly was in the... interview there.

JOHNSON   Okay. Uh the next question I have is uh... were you telling the truth when you gave that statement?

TETREAULT   Definitely.

JOHNSON   Okay. Okay thank you. Uh that is it.

TETREAULT   Perfect.

JOHNSON   That is it.

TETREAULT   Okay.

JOHNSON   Okay. I'll uh

TETREAULT   Oh

JOHNSON   escort you out.

TETREAULT	actually there's
JOHNSON	Oh go ahead.
TETREAULT	one more thing. In the interview I

said I wasn't sure when I was out on the ground and I said I wasn't sure if I pleaded for my life whatever and I said wouldn't go to the police.

JOHNSON	Mm hm.
TETREAULT	I remember I did do that.
JOHNSON	Okay.
TETREAULT	Yeah so um I remember saying hey

just take what you want I won't even go to the police whatever. So

JOHNSON	Okay.
TETREAULT	I did remember that now.
JOHNSON	Okay.
TETREAULT	So yeah.
JOHNSON	Good. Good. Anything else?
TETREAULT	No that's it.
JOHNSON	No. (Laughter)
JOHNSON	Okay. Okay.
TETREAULT	(Unintelligible) now.
JOHNSON	Then uh then we're concluded.
TETREAULT	Okay.
JOHNSON	And uh I'll escort you out the

building.

TETREAULT	Sounds good.
JOHNSON	And we'll talk about uh your new

address and whatnot uh outside of this room.

TETREAULT	Sure.
JOHNSON	Okay. Oh thanks. You didn't make

any notes?

TETREAULT	No I just (unintelligible)
JOHNSON	Okay.

TETREAULT	it.
JOHNSON	Fair enough.
TETREAULT	Remember everything. (Door opens and closes)

Elapsed time 01:58:30
Recording ends
Transcribed by: Bobbie
09 Sep 24

Appendix 4 – Media Appearances

- Dateline NBC - Deadly House of Cards - Aired on NBC – September 16, 2011

- The Fifth Estate - MURDER, he wrote - Aired on CBC – November 18, 2011

- 48 Hours Mystery – Screenplay for Murder - Aired on CBS – February 11, 2012

- Dates from Hell - Web of Seduction - Aired on Investigation Discovery – July 25, 2012

- I Survived... - Gilles, Angela and Richard, Jeffrey - Aired on Biography – October 21, 2012

- 48 Hours Hard Evidence - Screenplay for Murder - Aired on the TLC – January 12, 2013

- True Crime Canada - Inside The Mark Twitchell Case - Aired on CBC – September 10, 2013

- The Security Brief – Script for Murder - Aired on REELZ – January 13, 2016

- Global Edmonton News - TV Interview - Aired on Global Edmonton – January 29, 2016

- Alberta Primetime – TV Interview - Aired on CTV Two – March 23, 2016

Appendix 5 – "House of Cards" Script

INT. HOME OFFICE - NIGHT

ROGER; a man in his early 40's surfs the web nervously. His hands shake in eager nervousness, he keeps peeking around the edge of the screen to keep an eye on the hallway. He can see the glow of the living room TV from down the hall and hear it's programming.

The website on his computer screen is an online matchmaking service for people who want to cheat on their spouses. He's checking his email when a message shows up from a very attractive woman. It reads. "Hey sexy, all set for tonight? See you soon, can't wait."

Roger quickly erases his browsing history and shuts the computer down. He stands up, dressed for the gym with a racket in slip case. He moves down the hall and into the entry way of his front door where his wife and children casually watch him.

ROGER
Well I'm off. I shouldn't be too long, just-a couple of hours. I don't think Ken can keep up like he used to.

JENNY
Go easy on him, the last thing he needs is to throw *his* back out again before his vacation starts.

ROGER Ok. Bye kids.

KIDS (IN UNISON)

Bye dad.

EXT. STREET - CONTINUOUS

Roger closes the door and walks out to his car, putting *his* racket in the trunk and pulling out a duffle bag in the process. He gets into the driver seat and fumbles around as he changes in the front seat of *his* car from his gym clothes to a stylish collared shirt and jeans. His car starts and pulls away, headed for it's destination.

EXT. DIFFERENT HOUSE FRONT - CONTINUOUS

Roger pulls up to the house. The porch light is on. He checks his breath and straightens his hair in the mirror. He turns the car off, gets out of the vehicle and heads toward the front door. He's about 7 steps from the door when the unmistakable sound of a stun gun being fired explodes from the darkness. Roger loses all control of his muscles and hits the ground violently twitching and shaking. Before he has time to comprehend what's going on he gets clubbed in the back of the head and is knocked unconscious.

INT. STORAGE UNIT - NIGHT

Roger awakens with a splitting headache and a spell of dizziness. When his eyes adjust he takes stock of *his* situation.
His hands are completely wrapped *in* duct tape and he *is* also fully duct taped to a steel chair that is bolted to the

floor. There is a strip of duct tape across *his* mouth. He's in an 8 foot by 24 foot storage area. A car is parked inside and there's a work table against the wall with a laptop on it. The laptop has superhero stickers on the back in a specific pattern. A person dressed in a large black PVC apron, with gloves and sporting a black street hockey mask with yellow streaks across it painted to look *like* a bear claw scratch with the mouth cut out suddenly appears out of nowhere, startling Roger.

KILLER
Boo! Heeheeeheehehehe. Ok Roger, welcome to a little game of live or die. The process is really quite simple so pay very close attention because I don't enjoy repeating myself and if you make me do that, well . . .

The killer pulls out a large intimidating hunting knife that nearly sends Roger into hysterics.

KILLER
Ok settle down Roger. You have nothing to worry about yet. If you play by the rules, then you will *live.* If you don't, I'm going to cut you up into tiny pieces and they will never find the body. I'm going to ask you a series of questions and how you answer those questions is going to decide your fate.
I'm going to check your answers while you're sitting here and if I find out you lied to me on any particular point, I'm going to cut your nutsack off and show it to you, do you read me?

Roger nods frantically.

KILLER
Perfect. Let's start with an easy one.
What's your Cheating Hearts password?

ROGER
mmmpphhhpmhhh.

The killer *is* still looking at *his* laptop screen.

KILLER
Sorry what? I didn't *quite* catch that?

The killer looks back at Roger realizing the tape still covers
his mouth.

KILLER Oh, right. Sorry.

The Killer moves back over to Roger and grips the edge of
the duct tape, pauses and leanin to him.

KILLER
I realize this goes without saying but I don't want any
misunderstandings. If you scream I'm going to cut your
windpipe out which will cause an awfully huge mess and
leave you unable to answer any more questions so I'd
recommend you restrain yourself.

The killer rips the tape off Rogers mouth and wheels his
chair back over to the desk.

Password.

KILLER

ROGER
sixtyniner.

The killer stops, looks at *him* through the mask and then back at the screen. He sighs and starts typing.

KILLER
Very original dipshit.

The killer goes about deleting any messages from the fake female account he obviously created to lure Roger in and speaks at the same time.

KILLER
Roger you've chosen to cheat on your wife. You chose to betray the mother of your children by attempting to sleep around with some slut you've never even met. That's going to cost you. Email password please.

ROGER
golfwizard.

KILLER
My god you're a pussy.

Killer keeps going as he deletes all *evidence* from the victims *email* account.

KILLER
You could have contracted an STD or if your wife found out regardless you'd lose your house and half of your income for a very long time. But you chose to ignore the consequences and now I'm going to give you some. What's your wifes email address?

ROGER
jadeprincess at seamail dot com.

KILLER
I'm going to take you for whatever will come out of your bank account tonight and then let you re-enter your pathetic little life. Once you do, if you call the police or try to have me investigated I will make sure that your two children suffer in ways you couldn't possibly imagine before they die slowly and painfully at my own hand. And if you're thinking you'll call the cops incognito and under the radar, without the press being notified, don't bother. I work for the police, I'll know about it. You're also going to let karma takes its course. If you warn the other men on that site or anyone else for that matter about me and what I do, I'm going to shoot two completely random school children during their afternoon recess and leave a note from you taking credit for it. I already have your prints on the murder weapon.

Killer holds up the gun *in* a ziplock.

KILLER
Got em off you before I taped up your hands. So ...we have a Visa and a debit card. What's the debit pin number?

ROGER
two·zero seven six.

KILLER
Ok, you realize I'm going to test this in an ATM before I let you go *right?* Care to change your answer?

ROGER Nope, that's it.

KILLER
Good boy. You already made it farther than my last visitor.

Killer nods to a jar on a shelf where Roger sees a severed ear.

KILLER
What's the available balance on the Visa?

ROGER
Two thousand even.

The killer gets up and walks over to Roger and starts covering Rogers mouth and eyes with more duct tape.

KILLER
Ok Roger we're almost at the home stretch here. I'm going to take a very short trip to confirm these details. These doors lock from the outside and this whole building is sound proofed.

Killer now takes his mask off and begins_ to pack up his laptop and other items into a bag.

KILLER
If you try to escape and fail, I'll kill you when I get back. If by some insane miracle you're not here at all,
your children die tonight. Do we understand one another?

Roger nods quickly.

KILLER
Excellent. I will see you shortly.

The killer leaves and the padlock is heard closing behind him. A car starts and slowly drifts away. A cross fade shows *time* passage and the sound of a car pulling up *is* heard. The padlock is undone and the killer returns. He puts *his* mask back on and then takes the tape off Rogers eyes and mouth.

KILLER
Hi Roger, how are you?

Roger stares at him in disbelief.

KILLER
Listen I have good news and bad news. Which do you want first?

Good.

ROGER

KILLER
The good news is, everything went off

beat.

without a hitch, you played by the rules, which leads me to the bad news.

KILLER
I thought it over and it turns out I can't let you live after all.

Roger starts blubbering and begging for his life.

KILLER
Nope, no I'm sorry but it has to be this way. It just occurred to me I can't use framing you for murder as a reliable threat to keep my secret. After all a typed note and some prints on a weapon you didn't register are nothing against a rock solid alibi with witnesses from work or home and that's going to eventually unravel the truth about me one way or another. If you just disappear things will be a lot easier.

Killer moves to the wall where he takes down an exquisite folded steel samurai sword.

KILLER
My profile and emails don't exist in your world anymore. They'll just assume you ran off with one of your hussies and decided not to come back, especially when your wife finds an email from your email account confessing everything and telling her your plans. It happens every day. But you

know what Roger, it's better this way. Your wife won't have to live with a liar and a cheat for a husband and your kids will remember you as a good guy.

Roger twists and rocks in futility shaking his head and whining.

KILLER
Do you know what this is Roger? This is a work of art. Samurai swords have a history of taking out the trash my friend. They were once used to defend and regain honor from a place of dishonor. This is a perfectly tempered folded steel weapon, built for one purpose. Now they sit on the walls of collectors, but all they collect is dust. They're left to rot in some douchebags den while he plays video games at the end of a long hard day of licking his bosses ass and jerking off to some dirty magazines. But not this guy Roger. This one gets to fulfill it's purpose.

The killer winds up and decapitates Roger in one smooth motion. The head slumps to the floor and as the neck spurts blood, the killer casually cleans the blade and puts it back into the scabbard, replacing it on the wall. He then picks up a power saw and goes to town on dismembering the body off screen. When we come back to seeing the killer he's carefully packing the pieces into hefty bags and placing them in his trunk.

INT. HOME LIBRARY - DAY

A writer leans back from staring intensely at his laptop screen and puts his hands behind his head taking a deep sigh in relief that he's just finished something solid. He closes microsoft word and a website showing the inside workings of a female profile on a cheaters dating site is the last thing to shut down. He closes the laptop and the shell displays superhero stickers on it in a distinctive pattern. He puts it into his carrying case and leans over to close a duffel bag containing gloves, a stun gun and a black mouthless hockey mask with yellow streaks on it.

He moves to his living room and kisses his wife goodbye.

WIFE
Off to the gym honey? -

WRITER
You bet, gotta relieve some tension from sitting so long.

WIFE
How's the story coming along?

WRITER
Really well sweetie. It's true when they say the best way to succeed is to write what you know.

She smiles and he walks out the door. Fade to black

Appendix 6 – SKCONFESSIONS

This story is based on true events. The names and events were altered slightly to protect the guilty.

This is the story of my progression into becoming a serial killer. Like anyone just starting out in a new skill, I had a bit of trial and error in the beginning of my misadventures. Allow me to start from the beginning and I think you'll see what I mean.

I don't remember the exact place and time it was that I decided to become a serial killer but I remember the sensation that hit me when I committed to the decision. It was a rush of pure euphoria. I felt lighter, less stressed if you will at the freedom of the prospect. There was something about urgently exploring my dark side that greatly appealed to me and I'm such a methodical planner and thinker, the very challenge itself was enticing to behold.

This realization was just the last in a series of new discoveries I made about myself.

I just knew I was different somehow from the rest of humanity. I feel no such emotions as empathy or sympathy toward others for example.

Of course when it came to actual one on one conversations with therapists, I had to lie. I mean talk about leaving a trail of bread crumbs. The last thing I needed to do was air out all of my darkest fantasies and half formed plans to someone who is legally obligated to contact the authorities if they think a patient will do harm to themselves or others. I'm not stupid. Nevertheless, deception aside, it was a useful exercise to get to know my label better.

When a man approaches thirty years of age, he tends to question what his ultimate purpose is in this world and where he fits into the picture. And then I remembered something else. A passage I read from a novel by the renowned fantasy writer, David Gemmell in reference to a bronze age assassin. I can't recall the exact wording but it was the philosophy that hit home. The assassin reflected on what he does with his life with guilt (another emotion I am incapable of) and someone imparted a bigger picture wisdom.

He said that the assassin is the hand of fate. Fate has already decided everyone's time to die from the moment they are born. When it's their time, it's their time and if they do not die of old age or sickness, when their time comes other factors are employed by fate to get the job done. I think about that whenever I plan a kill. It's not me who chooses the victims but fate. Oh sure I choose the victim to match my own criteria in the interest of remaining free and at large, but for the most part I am merely following my own nature which was devised by the grand design of the universe.

Now this does not mean I shirk responsibility for my actions. I am very obviously, as you will come to learn, deliberate, level headed and very much in control of my own actions. Although I won't deny that the aforementioned scenario would play well in an insanity plea.

So here I was, armed with this new insight into my inner self and an exhilarating new hobby that I was seeking to undertake. I thought long and hard to come up with a system that would work for me, a method that would ensure I could have my play time and keep from getting caught. It didn't take long before I settled on an M.O.

I would use online dating to rope in my victims. Once I came up with that one clear starting point, all of the other pieces needed to be tended to. I began to ask myself a series of questions designed to get me to consider every possible angle. I wanted to have every step in the process already planned out from start to finish because improvising would be bad and lead to sloppiness. I had to have an order, a plan, something that would bring calm to a chaotic situation.

First question: Who do I want to target? At first I considered married men looking to cheat on their wives. In one way I'd be taking out the trash, doling out justice to those who on some level, deserved what they got. But the logic of the situation denies this possibility. After all people who are expected home at a certain hour tend to get reported as missing and there's other factors that would lead to an investigation I didn't want. No, I had to choose people whose entire lives I could infiltrate and eliminate evidence of my existence from on all levels.

I finally settled on middle-aged single men who lived alone. My reasons were numerous. For one thing, they would be easy to lead by their dicks, easy to manipulate, easy to

238

seduce under my fake female disguises. They were also the most likely targets to have the most expendable money in their bank accounts. A tidbit I would use to my advantage later on. Finally, by living alone, once they were out of the picture I could easily enter their living spaces undetected with no forced entry and remove all sorts of valuable items from the premises.

Oh yes my friend, I am in this for profit. It has always been my attitude that no hobby or venture should ever be done without expected return on investment.

For many years I crafted elaborate Halloween costumes, faithful screen accurate recreations of very big blockbuster movie icons. The result of my efforts in these costumes, were various 1st prizes in costume contests that resulted in cash payouts worth at least forty times what I spent to make each outfit. This would be no different.

I had expenses with this new hobby and I would make sure that I generated a profit from it to recoup and eclipse my costs. That was the next step in the process for being fully prepared, a detailed shopping list of all the items I would need to carry out my plans.

First off I needed a location. I scoured listings to find something suitable. I started looking in regular secure storage but the video surveillance and inability to get my victims there smoothly threw that idea out the window quickly. When I finally found my location it could not have been any more perfect.

A double detached garage for rent in the south of the city, tucked away in a quiet neighborhood on a lot with a house occupied by tenants who couldn't even read English, much less speak it, no doubt work program immigrants brought in by a donut chain with supplied housing.

Everything, I decided, would take place here. The approach, the apprehension and the kill as well as preparation for disposal of the body could all be done in relative seclusion from this one building. Total privacy. I immediately went to work removing the address plank from the back, blocking out all the windows with boards and duct tape, replacing locks.

The back driveway wasn't even paved, it was just a bed of gravel with grass growing out of it. The entire surrounding area was blocked out of sight from neighbors with high thick fences and the entire block was dead starting at eight o'clock at night.

My shopping list was very thorough. I went out to several different stores to avoid buying all of my items from one location and I paid cash to avoid a paper trail just in case. A street hockey mask, that I would soon cut the mouth out of and paint gold streaks into for dramatic effect. A basic dark green hoody, something comfortable with pockets that hides distinctive marks, body type and hair. Two sets of disposable overalls for what was sure to be a messy clean up process and I would use the plastic bags all this came in to wrap my shoes for the process.

I bought a hunters game processing kit, which if you think about it is ideal for this scenario. Why not use a whole set of tools designed to take apart large mammals in the forest on the fly? It reduces the spatter caused by power tools, takes the noise level way down too and there's also just something more gratifying about sawing through tendons and bone with your bare hands than using something else that takes the fun out of the work.

My kill knife was different though. I wanted the weapon used for the deed itself to be simple, elegant and beautiful in it's own way so I dropped by a military surplus store and picked up a well crafted hunting knife with an 8 inch blade. I would use this weapon to cleanly and simply slice open a gash in the victims neck allowing them to bleed out quickly and with no pain. I'm not a torture guy. Again, the noise level from the screams is not my thing at all and I only resort to that if they are still alive after apprehension but won't give me the simple information I ask for.

Several rolls of painters plastic sheeting to prep my kill room. At least 6 rolls of packing tape and just as many rolls of duct tape as well as two boxes of contractor grade hefty bags. I picked up a stun baton because I thought that would render my targets without use of their muscles quickly and painlessly and I bought an extra realistic airsoft pistol; something that could very easily be mistaken for the real thing, especially in low light just for that extra edge.

I made sure to acquire construction materials for my custom furniture. I went to town designing and building a rather sturdy four foot by six foot six inch table with stainless steel finish and angle iron edging. I also welded a rather mean looking chair and another table was left there by the realty company, which I used to stay organized on.

Finally I ordered a forty five gallon steel drum which would be the final resting place for the body parts before I incinerated them. I was all set, prepared as I could be. I diligently set up my kill room, creating the plastic bubble I needed to create my nasty mayhem. The trap was set, and now it was time to bait the hook.

I downloaded an IP address blocker first and foremost. I mean it would be rather silly of me to run this whole operation from my home computer without it, just so that if any of my play mates disappearances were ever actually investigated, there would be this electronic trail leading the police directly back to me and my little workshop of horrors.

Once activated, I created all new email addresses and dating site profiles for my dark plan. It was so easy it was almost insulting. But really, who thinks to look outside their pond when they go out fishing? No one. I did a quick search for females that matched what I wanted to represent in other cities around the world and when I found someone I liked, I copied their photos and used them in my new online identity as whoever it was I wanted to be.

I always change things up. I never use the same profile for more than one victim at a time, and I generate new email addresses as well, just in case. After a victim is removed from the world neatly and cleanly, I erase my accounts and every trace they left behind. Sure the mother servers may or may not have an imprinted image, but even if they checked, they wouldn't trace me.

As soon as the profiles go up, within twenty four hours the responses come in like a flood. I review the messages sent and choose my victims based on age, body type, profession, status and living situation. Obviously I'm not going to pursue a 6'4 athletic martial arts instructor who's married with 4 kids. That's just got trouble written all over it. I mean I'm ruthless but I'm not an idiot. I have my own fight training background but I don't have delusions of grandeur.

When I come across a single man in his late thirties to early forties who is self employed, lives alone and stands between 5'7 and 5'11 with an average body type weighing in between 150 and 180 lbs, I know I've found my ideal target.

Such was the case with a man I will refer to as Frank. That of course is not his real name and I won't divulge any other sensitive details about the situation but Frank was my very first target ever. I roped him in with a profile I was quite proud of featuring photos of a blonde I would like to bang myself.

I asked him to pick me up from my residence at a prescribed time on a particular night of the week and then gave him detailed instructions on how to find the place. I gave him some song and dance routine about how my landlord had the property setup to where the back gate was broken and padlocked and there was nowhere in front to park because of a no parking zone and a bus stop across the street. So I told him I would leave the garage door open for him to come in through and then to come the back door of the house, all the while realizing of course that he would never make it that far.

So the message was received and confirmed, and I waited.

Generally I was quite pleased with myself. I had a perfectly formulated plan, and I was fully prepared. I adorned my specialty mask, serving the double purpose of facial protection and identity shield to give the victim a false sense of security in thinking they would be let go since I cared about hiding who I was. But without explaining it to them, that thought would not likely cross their mind in the heat of the moment.

I slipped my hoody on and pulled the hood over my head, resting it comfortably over my brow. I slipped the knife holster with the blade in it onto my belt and pulled on my fine leather gloves.

My kill room was perfectly prepped. Plastic sheeting taped together and around my table; a large green cloth screwed into the drywall ceiling to shield view of it from my guests line of sight, and to shield me too of course. I now stood but a few feet away from the front door which I had locked of course. The plan was to wait in the shadow of my curtain until he approached the door and shock him with the stun baton followed by a sleeper hold that would sap away his consciousness so that I could tape him up and set him on my table.

The last thought that crossed my mind before Frank pulled up into the driveway had nothing to do with the event itself, but rather was a mental note that I would need to remember to get a stock of paper towels for miscellaneous clean up in the future.

The cars engine rumbled and its headlights shone bright in the lowering dusk. I thought if his headlights were on a delay self shut off like mine that he would see more than I wanted him to which still wasn't much. Just a few crates of tools and paint cans, normal garage accessories in my opinion. But his headlights turned off as his engine petered out. I heard the sound of the car door opening and closing and then the footsteps that followed.

My head was rushed with adrenaline, my stomach had a half second flutter of butterflies before my resolve strengthened and I stood there, ominous in the dark prepared to strike with my stun baton fully extended and the safety off.

The typical taser guns used by police carry a charge of 50,000 volts and we've seen what they do to the people hit with them. The stun baton boasts 800,000 volts which sounds practically lethal but you have to understand that it isn't the voltage but the amps delivered by the weapon that matter. Either way I was confident in the weapons strength.

My confidence was misplaced.

I took two swift silent steps toward my target and pressing the baton across the back of his neck, pulled the trigger. It shocked and jumped but did little more than merely alert the bastard to what was really going on. It did not render his muscles unusable and the little shit fought back.

I had a distinct advantage. I was taller and outclassed him in tenacity and strength. This was also my environment and he wasn't expecting to run into a psycho in a mask, only a beautiful woman he hoped he would get lucky with. The confusion played to my benefit and I struck him repeatedly. He yelled "what the fuck" at the top of his lungs. The noise was something I had hoped to avoid but I paid it no mind and continued attempting to subdue this defiant little shit.

I dropped the baton and punched him several times in the side of the head but still he would not go down. He broke free and I could tell he would make for the door, for the way he came in so I reached into my pocket and withdrew the gun.

I pointed it straight at him and all of a sudden he took me seriously, his eyes wide. I commanded him to get down on the floor, to which he obeyed quickly. If he lifted his head even the slightest bit I warned him against it. I removed my gloves and went for the duct tape. I tore a piece off and slipped it over his eyes.

It was then that I told him that if he did what I told him to, that I would let him live. I brought one arm down around his back and was reaching for the other arm when he began defying me again.

"No, I can't, I can't do this." He began. Retrospect is of course 20/20 and had I been able to go back to that moment there would have been a hundred things I would have done differently. Obviously overestimating the stun baton is a mistake I would not repeat. The other one was putting up with his bullshit. I should have just pounded him in the back of the head while he was down until he lay unconscious on the floor. I should have shut the big door when I had the chance but everything moved too quickly and I didn't want to take my eyes off him for one second.

He got back to his feet having removed the duct tape and when I pointed the gun at him again, he grabbed it. He gripped down hard, twice and I think I might have seen a gleam in him that indicated he felt the guns construction and realized it was not real but I can't be sure. I still held on for dear life, not willing to give him a blunt object to hit me back with.

Frank made a few feeble attempts to hit me and tried one impotent kick aimed at my groin that I easily deflected. I delivered a head butt to his face and he broke free again. I clutched onto his jacket but he shook himself loose of it and took off for the opening in the door.

He made it into the driveway and that's when I knew I was pooched. I followed him out, not caring anymore who might see me. He was fumbling on the ground. I grabbed him by the leg as if to drag him back into the garage caveman style but my energy was depleting and the human survival instinct is one of the most powerful forces on Earth. He tried to grab at my mask and came quite close to pulling it off. I broke the grasp and he spun away into the alley and sure enough, a couple on an evening stroll saw me coming after him sporting a deer in the headlight look that can only be described as a total lack of comprehension. I stared back at them through my mask for half a moment and then headed back for the cover of my lair.

I don't know why I played it as cool as I did. Maybe it was something Frank said during the skirmish about swearing not to tell anyone if I let him go. Maybe it was my own instincts about reading people and the fear in his eyes that told me deep down, he wouldn't report the incident, but I felt ok.

I still packed any gear up of my own and his stray jacket into a bag. Whatever I felt like keeping I cleaned prints off of and tossed the rest in a dumpster. As a final touch I sent one last warning email to Frank through the dating site telling him I had traced his IP address through his messages and that if he did report me, I would hunt him down where he lives when he least expects it and finish what I started. I threw in a line about having cased the garage, that it wasn't even mine and that I never use the same location twice. My last lie was to tell him he was lucky number eighteen on my spree.

I wasn't sure if I should believe it worked. I walked calmly out to my car, got in and drove away, across the entire city back to my home where my wife and child waited for me. During the entire trip I kept thinking surely this douche bag would call the police. Not that it mattered if he did. I covered my tracks well.

248

You see in my day life I'm an independent film-maker and everything in that garage could be easily explained away as props for filming a psychological thriller. How I could be on one side of the city scrapping with a potential kill up until 7:20pm and be home less than an hour later would have been a stretch at best.

Still, I couldn't shake the foreboding feeling. I kept thinking any moment I'd see flashing lights behind me asking me to pull over, despite my perfect adherence to posted speed limits and cautious observance of the safety belt law. Surely the arresting officer would wonder why I was so sweaty and why there was a bag with a hoody, a jacket, a prohibited stun weapon and a set of handcuffs in my trunk.

But those lights never showed up in my rear view mirror.

I checked my voicemail messages and had two; very unusual this time of night. One from my wife wondering if I could be home by 8:30 so that she could pick up a package before 9:00 and one from my prop guy asking if he could borrow my airsoft pistol. Paranoia set in. My wife wouldn't care about picking up a package this late, she'd wait until tomorrow. Could the cops have gotten to her and convinced her to pretend to get me home quicker so they could arrest me?

But I had to stop and think clearly. This was all happening way too fast. There's no way that was possible, this wasn't a movie, this was real life. Even if the police were contacted, their response time to the location would be in the neighborhood of twenty minutes to two hours and there'd be no way for them to verify who rented the garage that quickly.

My fear subsided and I drove home. I practiced my entire behavior pattern should I come home to police cruisers parked along my front yard. I would rush the door in a panic and upon entering or being stopped by patrolmen I would appear utterly surprised and beg them to know if anything had happened to my precious wife and/or daughter. My genuine shock of their presence would start me on the innocent path in their eyes, and then my cover story of being at a therapy appointment would become my short term alibi until I could confess to the cops later that therapy was a cover story I gave my wife so I could have just one night a week to myself.

Between that and the total lack of hard evidence I'd be free regardless and yet still the nervousness set in.

It's pretty fucking hard to concentrate on anything when you live in constant expectation of the police arriving at your doorstep. It turns out my wife did need to pick up a package, a pilates chair that she wanted me to assemble. The directions couldn't be any more complicated than the directions for making mac and cheese but I had a really hard time because the apprehension was always there.

Every time I heard a car drive by I'd feel compelled to look out the window. I heard a massive group of sirens get closer, and closer and closer. My heart leaped into my chest until I realized there was a house fire somewhere close to the area.

Seeing a police cruiser slowly and deliberately pull around my block was the worst part. But then I remembered our across the street neighbor had an itchy trigger finger for calling the cops when the rowdy teenagers next door partied too loudly and it subsided.

A day passed. I spent that day with my 8 month old daughter as my wife ran errands and kept appointments. Then the day turned to night and once again I was suspicious but nothing happened. That was the night I was totally convinced I had gotten off on this one pretty much scot free.

No patrol car would come to take me away bound in handcuffs to be brought up on assault charges, forever ending my serial killing career before it began and bringing down my marriage with it when my wife finds out what I really am.

That first time experience was the basis for my revised method of opperandi. Previously I wanted my victims alive and conscious after I had subdued them. I wanted to get information from them like their email and dating site passwords as well as the pin codes to their debit cards and credit cards. But this priority is now a distant second to making sure I don't get caught. I got lucky that first time and I wasn't going to assume that would ever happen again if anyone else got loose.

So I had to revise my apprehension system in order for it to go more smoothly. I decided to ramp up the savagery of my attack, leaving no margin for error in rendering a target unconscious within the first ten seconds. I dropped the stun baton for the favor of two 24 inch lengths of galvanized steel piping. I was confident that swinging for the fences to the back of the head would do the trick. I would go on a shopping trip the next day to make it happen.

> Chapter break

Oh my sweet Laci. Just in case you are wondering, Laci is not my wife, or my daughter. Laci is my ex girlfriend. On paper she's the complete opposite of everything that should be my perfect match. She has two small dogs that she treats like human children and those people usually drive me up the wall.

She's also periodically depressed and suffers from frequent anxiety attacks whereas I usually prefer a much more together woman. All these things exist but I love her uncontrollably and always will.

Laci and I met in my first year of college. I was 19 at the time and unbeknownst to me at the time she was 24. I've always been into older women. The first time I met her I was waiting outside the door of an English class I didn't need to take since the school had just dropped the required grade for my program the night before. Still, I thought it couldn't hurt to ride the class out since I had already paid for it and would possibly use the higher mark for something else in the future.

I sat on the floor writing a story. Laci sat down across from me and simply said "Hi." I said hi back and that was the beginning of the end for us.

Our relationship is always and forever on unstable ground. When we first met she was just trying to be friendly but she had a boyfriend. A very stiff, unemotional, dependable long term boyfriend. I was too young and naive to know where this was headed.

I lied to her from the onset. I lied to her about my heritage and my age. Stupid basic life things that are completely pointless to lie about but I did it anyway. Part of me was insecure about just being myself but part of me also didn't think this relationship would go anywhere since she was taken.

I was wrong. It went somewhere very quickly. We became fast friends, she wanted to be in the story I was writing. We began hanging out on a regular basis. I had lied to her about having a girlfriend myself so as not to appear single and therefore, pathetic. So it was really rather easy for me to show up to class one day pretending to be distraught over my girlfriend having dumped me. That day our friendship grew into something stronger.

We spent more time together, very often curling up on a couch as just friends, while we watched TV and nuzzled. Friends rubbed their faces together affectionately didn't they? These ones did, at least until one night when we couldn't take it anymore and made out like a couple of teenagers, which technically speaking I still was.

It was a long hard complicated battle over the next several months as she hummed and hawed over what to do. She was a serial dater to my future serial killer and had never taken down time between relationships, always afraid to be alone. Eventually she did in fact dump her boyfriend for me but the fast transition left damage. She would act out in inappropriate ways, kiss another guy and then say she had to in order to see if what we had was real.

It was no worse than what I had done to her of course. Toward the end of our relationship she also began to find religion and I knew the end was nigh. It's not that I have a problem with religious people per se, I have some very good friends who are quite religious. It's just that I could see major issues down the line with butting heads over what to teach our kids or how to live our lives. Not to mention the fact that killing people isn't exactly welcomed in the kingdom of the man made, 'make me feel better about myself through guilt' system of the faithful.

I didn't need to wait for any of these issues to wreck our relationship. Eventually one lie after another began to unravel. First at my birthday party when my age was revealed to be a year younger than I told her, and then the death blow when she flat out asked my parents about the family origins in the car one day.

Dishonesty had taken its toll and Laci decided to end the relationship. I was absolutely devastated. Crushed beyond all reckoning. I lost my soul mate, the one true love of my life and would never get over it. I told her as I left that night that I love her more than anyone I've ever loved, that I will never love anyone the same way again and that no one she ever meets will lover her with the same intensity, passion and commitment that I do.

Laci tried to tell me I cared for women too much and that I would find someone else. It was remarkable how right I was and how wrong she was about the entire situation.

For eight years I thought about her constantly. Several times I tried to touch base with her to see how she was doing. At one point I made brief contact after I found her in a hotmail member search but she cut things off sharply and quickly, said she was getting engaged and that was it.

I would soon come to find out she hadn't written those responses, but her friend did on her behalf and two weeks later, Laci had changed her mind and wanted to get together but she never reconnected with me.
I went through one failed marriage in the meantime, and so did she. When Laci and I reconnected through a social networking website, she was just in the process of getting divorced, ironically from a total sociopath who drained her of all her self worth. Years of neglect and mistreatment at the hands of a negative, unaffectionate douchebag who would rather play a video game than be intimate with her had taken it's toll.

By the time I found her again, Laci had forgotten what it had been like to be in a caring loving relationship. Her self esteem had been torn to shreds and she had turn to the unconditional love of her animals to keep her going.

By this time I was already married for the second time, to a wonderful woman. Tess was everything I needed to balance my life out. She kept me on my toes and organized. She was a very high stress person with a lot of tension and I mellowed her out too. We had hit it off from the beginning, found what I thought was love and gone on to be married and have our daughter together, beautiful Zoe.

I even gave Tess the Laci test. I coined this after years of finding the way to figure out if a relationship was worth keeping or not. I would simply ask myself "If Laci walked into my life and asked me to run away with her, would I do it?"

If the answer was yes, then I should end my relationship. If the answer was no, I finally found true love. With Tess, I answered no so the next logical choice was to ask her to marry me. What I didn't count on was finding Laci again ... through Facebook.

It started out as a congratulations on each others happiness, which led to a meeting, which led to feelings which then led to an intense make out session in a local restaurant. Every feeling I had for Laci came flooding back to me. The strength of love, the adoration, all of it; it was like a tidal wave crashing through me.

Tess was 3 months pregnant with Zoe at the time and I had a panick attack. A huge conflict of motivation, obligation and sense of duty overcame me and I actually felt guilt. Like an idiot I confessed everything to Tess the next day thereby destroying the trust in our relationship. Trust is all anyone has in a relationship and it's the one pillar everything else is based around. Mess with that and you end your world.

This did not happen amazingly. Tess is a very strong, independent person with very strong opinions on morals and ethics. I was certain she'd dump me, pregnant or not but she didn't. She made a conscious choice to forgive me, accept my temporary insanity plea and trust me again.

Ending things with Laci after promising her I would leave Tess for her resulted badly. There was anger, frustration and heartache. I was blocked on Facebook for a long time. A year in fact. I had all but lost any hope of ever hearing from Laci again. And then I got the strangest email.

Laci sent me a message on Facebook asking to be friends again. She was engaged again to some other sociopathic douche and just like last time, she was on the verge of ending it. He was just another neglectful, self serving, immature limp fish who had disappointed her for the last time with his philandering and mistreatment of her.

We quickly began a dialogue and although I told my wife Laci had emailed me, I also told her that I deleted the message and ignored her. That was obviously a lie. Tables had turned. Laci knew more about me and my situation than Tess did. It wasn't fair to her but she was also in the dark, which was better for her all around.

I started seeing Laci again. First it was innocent little coffee dates and movies. We went to see a horror film, something low budget and shot entirely hand held as was the Hollywood fad at the time and we maybe caught 20 minutes of a 90 minute movie between all the intense kissing we were doing.

It was the first week of October and I had always done something very elaborate for Halloween. Laci wanted to join me for Halloween, get a hotel and spend the entire day having sex. I was all about it but I knew there was no way I could wait that long. The engine in the back of my head that makes things happen started planning and plotting immediately on how to make this happen. Only problem was, she lived about an hour out of town and logistics were difficult to manage.

I would come back to this problem later, right now I had someone to kill and some new methods to try out.

I went to my neighborhood Home Depot to find what I needed and sure enough, in the plumbing section there they were; two galvanized steel pipes. I thought it might do to pick up some hockey tape while I was there in order to create a better grip on one side.

I rounded the aisle just in time to see a daddy daughter team shopping for plumbing accessories, no doubt for their original intended use. The little girl couldn't have been any older than five and had found the stick portion of a toilet plunger without it's companion on the end. She wielded it like a sword and held a defensive pose, quite expertly I might add.

Ordinarily I'm somewhat irritated by children but when they do something stunningly mature for their age or endearing to my heart I can't help but smile and smile I did at this feisty little sweetheart who I hoped would be Zoe in 4 years.

The girl grinned sheepishly back at me. Her smile revealed her thoughts. She was smiling with a face that said "I'm a little embarrassed that you caught me but you seem to think it's cool so I'll return the devilish grin you're giving me." I think the young lady and I shared a moment just then.

I strolled out into the parking lot and got back into the comfy me shaped indent in the front seat of my maroon sedan. I wrapped the pipe ends in hockey tape for optimal gripping. Satisfied with this, I went home to relax and to set up my next victim.

The cool thing about a seven month old is that you can openly tell them anything and they can't rat you out. I needed that from my daughter, since anyone else I could spill to would be dialing nine one one before I finished. I knew I only had a limited amount of time before Zoes comprehension got to the level where that wouldn't fly so I got in as much talk time as possible in her early development when the words were just soothing sounds to get her used to the English language.

>break.

I'm a huge fan of the Showtime series Dexter, as you may have guessed if you're at all familiar with the show. Dexter enjoys the sweet dark alone time of his own apartment since his TV girlfriend Rita and her two kids, Astor and Cody are not as tangled into his life as my family is with mine. I had to do with the sweet dark alone time of my basement computer office.

Once the child was snugly tucked away in her crib and my wife was sleeping peacefully, it sufficed perfectly for what I needed to do. My wife is certainly no sound sleeper, requiring ear plugs just to conk out and getting up several times during the night but we sleep apart so my disturbing her from getting up was never an issue.

Some people think that sleeping apart is detrimental to the relationship. I don't see how. I mean I'm only a serial killer, seeing my ex girlfriend on the side and my wife has no clue about it. But neither of those things has to do with the sleeping arrangements in our household. I sleep in the basement because I often stay up later than my wife and when we do sleep together, there's never enough room in a queen bed for two. Eventually the kicking and blanket hogging had us re-evaluate the importance of sharing a mattress.

I fired up my IP address blocker and launched two windows for my dual purpose. Keeping to my rules of never using the same account twice for anything, I opened a brand new email account. I stuck to the majors. Hotmail, Yahoo, Gmail. Something generic. When choosing a username it always reflected my new alias in some way. If I was an immigrant from Ireland looking for guys with a thing for redheads I'd use a username to the effect of lrishfirecream or something else just as apt.

Once the account had been created I used the second window to launch the dating site of choice. I switched that up to keep it interesting as well. Sometimes I would use a basic free service, and sometime I would use an elaborate pay service. It never mattered because women never have to pay to use those sites anyways. It's the horny retards on the other end who let their dicks dreams open their wallets.

On this night, a Thursday, I decided on a free site. Now photos are important. A photo of a girl that looks too professional gets overlooked because it reeks of spam bot. It also causes the guys to ask for more photos, which I would of course not have and would be forced to start from scratch.

A handy trick I use is to steal other women's photos from the same site, but in a different city. So if I posted my profile originating from say Portland, I would do a quick search in Nashville first and find a woman who I would genuinely be attracted to. Someone who doesn't come off as a total slut, but who also doesn't exude prude either. In this case I went ahead and chose the redhead from Ireland going out of country entirely for the photos.

Writing a womans dating profile is very simple. You read enough and they all start to sound the same after awhile. I wrote delicately, sweetly, as a woman would write. I listed a few of the things my new persona was not interested in and made a few kind comments at the end and an invitation to message me.

This profile was listed looking for 'dating', which is much more manageable than 'intimate encounter'. When looking for dating I only had to sift through less than thirty emails throughout the day. But when putting 'intimate encounter' it's more like thirty messages per hour, sometimes more. That can be good or bad depending on what you're looking for.

I was looking for someone to match my needs for a new victim. I wanted a man who was financially stable, lived alone, didn't answer to too many people and might have some time off coming up. I got exactly what I was looking for.

Amongst the smart assed punks and the creepy old fellas who frankly, would be more suspicious of me if I gave them the time of day than not based on their appearances, was my target. A six footish seemingly nice man who appeared clean cut, not overly good looking but not an ogre either and most importantly, fit for the profile.

We exchanged messages back and forth but when it came time to move in for the invite, another curve ball came my way. He wasn't available Friday, only Saturday. I had put in too much time with this asshole to start over and my mind began to race about how to fit it in.

I chose Fridays because I had a fake appointment with an imaginary psychiatrist who I told my wife I was seeing to sort out some of my issues, although I had already done that some time before. It was a very convenient and perfectly credible cover story though and I saw the merit in keeping the illusion going for the purpose of my late night freedom.

So every Friday I would leave the house, and prep for a kill while my wife was convinced my shrink was working his magic. I even added the special performance of seeming lighter and more relaxed when I walked back into the house. It was only partially an act since I did in fact feel good about my evening, just not in the way Tess quite expected.

Starting a kill on a Friday works on so many levels. For one thing, most people are not hard and fast expected to be anywhere on the weekend which gives me three days to clean up and tie up the loose ends. For another, I ordinarily need to skulk around doing my dirty work in the dead of night after Tess and Zoe are fast asleep. With all that night activity I get pretty bagged during the day so it's nice to not have career obligations on top of a lack of sleep.

I wasn't quite sure how to deal with my new friends schedule change. I thought to myself that starting over and slamming on the gas with a different profile entirely in order to stick to plan would have been the best idea. But I had already groomed this guy and felt profile mattered more than time of day.

I decided to leave it open and sleep on it, deciding what to do in the morning. Friday morning came and my decision was made. I would scrap yesterdays escapade and start over fresh. I found some new photos of a girl from L.A. and whipped up an intimate encounter profile. Something quick and dirty and to the point. She was on the prowl and looking to hook up that very night, my chosen night.

Then something happened I did not expect; a pleasant surprise among the scads of emails from young douchebags with no appeal at all and some flaming rude comments at the ready. I got a message from Mr. Thursday.

It seemed that he was not only a liar but a wannabe player as well. He lied to my other dummy account about being tied up Friday and was seeking something with more immediate gratification for the time being. It was all I needed to see.

I flirted back and forth like it was an art form. Finally when enough messages had been exchanged and I felt comfortable with his comfort level I invited him in. It crossed my mind to use my other account to message him and entice him into this night as well just to watch him squirm but I would watch him squirm plenty in person.

I gave him step by step directions to my kill room without revealing an address and making sure to include the general excuses about the bus stop in front of the place and the lack of parking. He bought it hook line and sinker. The time was set. 7:00pm.

My kill room was still perfectly set up from the last time, plastic sheeting hanging from the walls, on the floor and of course around my glorious table, duct tape sealing the seams to create a bubble to work within. I put that useless stun baton away and stretched my body out to limber up. I donned my mask, pulled my hood up and waited. The lights were still on inside the garage. It was 6:47 and I had a little time yet so I got myself psyched up for the main event.

Suddenly I heard the rumble of a car engine and sharply turned to see the wheel base of a Mazda slow and then continue. My adrenaline soared. That was him. The bastard was early and I know he had to have seen my feet at the very least. I decided to stick to the pattern anyway. I shut the lights all down and waited behind the curtain I had rigged up to shield me from sight; my two pipes in hand.

I ran entirely on sounds now. The cars engine silencing. The brief pause where all I could hear was the distant sound of main drag traffic lightly dancing in the background. Then the door opened, footsteps followed and then the car door slammed shut.

Another pause.

I could hear the crinkle of his clothing as he crouched to get under the door. He stood up and said "Hello?"

I froze. This was new. I've never heard anyone call out hello to a black empty room before. He assumed I was still here, and he was right. After all I had told him under my alias that there would be a guy using the garage for the weekend as a workshop.

I quickly took the mask off setting it on the weaker secondary table I used for my laptop. And without any other plan I began acting again.

"Hello?" I called back in a cheerful tone. I moved to the light switches and illuminated the room. "I'm Harry" I said pointedly, not sure what else to say exactly. "I'm a local film maker, preparing a set that's supposed to look like a serial killers little area here. You might have heard of my stuff. I'm the guy who put together the comedy feature at our local film festival."

"I haven't heard of that." replied the man who I will refer to from now on as Jim.

I went into super friendly mode, showed him my prop gun and how it wasn't real. I quickly mentioned that his date was running a little late and would be back in about twenty minutes. He said he would come back.

For twenty minutes I paced back and forth considering what to do, weighing the risks and the benefits. He could be on the phone to one of his friends revealing the address and telling them all about my set up. On the other hand he knows me so now I have an advantage over him and simultaneously, an obligation to use that advantage to remove him from the picture.

Still when my twenty minutes were up, I chickened out. As his car pulled up for the second time I whipped out my cell phone and in another grand performance pretended to talk to my alias over the phone. I delivered the bad news that tragically it looked like she wasn't going to be able to make it.

"I'm sorry bud, I don't know how long you had to drive to get here (27 blocks total, 10 minutes tops including lights) but it sounds like she's stuck in traffic and has no idea how long she'll be."

And with that, my victim left. He walked right out the door that should've been closing on his doom right then. I took stock of my situation. I was standing in the middle of a perfectly prepped kill room and was actually going to let this go down as strike 2. I already had the room set up and the whole night was mine to do with as I pleased so I jumped back online to find someone who was willing to drop everything and head over right away.

My new account which I had just created that morning had clear over 200 messages from all sorts of people. After twenty five minutes of perusing I still had nothing when my twice escaped victim sent me a message. My immediate reply was a huge apology and an offer to reschedule for the next day.

His reply was to come over again that very night. He didn't live far and didn't want to waste his night any more than I wanted to waste mine. I stared at the laptop screen, unmoving for half an hour deciding. Humming and hawing over the details. Finally I went for it. I typed a message back with a quick apology for the delay and an invitation to come back. I meant business.

Crouched, poised, I had a whole new plan. No mask needed this time. Just pretending to be poking around at the back of the set and then WHAM! I would slam him unconscious and his survival would be a bonus, but not necessary. He played into it perfectly. He reappeared through the garage door and I soon followed.

"I guess I'm just a glutton for punishment" he shrugged. "You have no idea."

The room filled with the echo of the pipe crashing into the back of his skull as I could feel my predator self take over. That one single motion was the end all be all. I had committed now and there was no going back. The jig was up and it was kill or get arrested for aggravated assault with a deadly weapon, maybe even attempted murder.

I won't go to jail for an almost. But the son of a bitch didn't drop like the sack of potatoes I was expecting. Are you serious? I asked myself. I continued thwacking Jim over the head repeatedly but it only seemed to fuel his adrenaline too.

He began screaming at the top of his lungs. "Police! Police! Police!" and I just about shat my pants. My fury doubled and I blasted him so hard blood spattered everywhere, but primarily on me. He hit the floor but was still conscious.

Just like they all do, he offered money immediately. I always find this a little degrading for both my victim and myself. Like I couldn't just kill them and take it anyway. No please Mr. victim, give me some petty cash from your wallet and run along to the cops only to lead them back here. Ridiculous.

I paused for a minute. "You promise?" I said.

"Yes just please stop hitting me, oh my skull." Was his reply. And then in the instant he had to think about it I wailed on him again. Despite receiving several mortal blows to the head, the shock and adrenaline of the situation gave him the fire to fight back a little.

"I've had enough of this." He said as he feebly and dizzily tried to grab the pipe away from me. My anger resurged, I wrestled it from him and that was the last straw for me. I pulled my hunting knife from it's sheath and watching the shock on his face as he saw the blade, I thrust it into his gut. His reaction was pure Hollywood. The lurch forward with the grunt was dead on TV movie of the week.

I didn't even notice the garage door was still part open. Wasn't I suppose to close that? Will I never learn?

No one came. No one rustled, not even from across the alley. My little notices that I sent out to the neighbors about shooting thrillers here did their job and no one paid attention, assuming it was a scene or something. Oh it was a scene alright.

Jim moaned and groaned. I plunged the knife deep into his neck. Days after the event I would reflect on this and wish I had tricked him by offering to call an ambulance if he just gave me his debit pin code before I sliced open his jugular.

269

Maybe I'll save that for the next victim since they never seem to just fall the fuck asleep like they're supposed to.

I led him bleed out right there on the floor, away from the plastic sheeting specifically put up to avoid that sort of thing. But hey I had bigger problems. I had no real idea if a jogger, a dog walker, an unconvinced neighbor or some other random individual had actually called the cops, just as a precaution.

I was standing there covered in blood. It was all over my face, my hoody, my coat and my jeans. I was holding the murder weapon in my hand standing over what would be in moments, a corpse and not nearly enough time to make it go away.

I got my things ready and did the only thing I could do. I waited. I waited for a sign on what to do next. I waited for the fast approach of sirens as a cue to leave and come up with a damn good story for later. I waited and I was rewarded with silence. Sweet sweet silence. I got lucky. No one freaked out, no one reacted, no one inadvertently witnessed it and no one called the boys in blue. I was home free.

I assessed my situation and went to town on my improvised solution. I had a dead guy that needed processing so that's what I did. I processed him.

I remember thinking as I hoisted this giant up onto my table that I should really stick to smaller guys from now on. This guy was at least 2 inches taller than I was and maybe a couple of pounds heavier, and I'm no shrimp.

But I got his dead carcass up on that table and I figured that since I went through all this trouble and made all this mess that I would have to clean up, I got my game processing kit out which contained a butcher knife for the hefty meat, a fillet knife for smaller works, a skinner which might come in handy for scalping the skull, and a serrated saw for the bones. A pair of scissors there was also and a cutting board. I had the cleaver there from another order I had placed.

I decided the best course would be to go from the feet up. First things first, I pulled out his wallet and keys and placed them on my computer table. Then I used the scissors to cut his pants apart and pull them away. I had my 45 gallon steel drum host to a contractor grade hefty bag where I was putting all the items. I cut the shirt off too but left the underwear. I don't need to see my kills dead junk hanging out while I'm trying to work.

I poked and prodded the joints to find the path of least resistance. I began cutting the legs off at the knees, all in one piece. I didn't even bother to take his shoes or socks off. The knife went through flesh like it was nothing. I was surprised at how utterly non resilient human tissue can be. Even the tendons and ligaments separated cleanly.

There was almost no blood. Not surprising since the grand majority of it was pooled on the floor, thankfully soaked up primarily by Jims jacket which had come off during our struggle.

I put the severed leg in the trash and moved on to the thigh which was essentially the same routine, only thicker, more fatty. I noticed that it wasn't nearly as horrendous as the media made it look on TV or in movies. Dismembering a human body was a relatively unexciting event. But I had my ways of making it more fun. I sang to myself as I worked, talked to myself, reflected on the new tools I would get to make the next one easier.

I took the arms off at the elbow joint and used the scissors to cut off fingertips for added confusion in identifying the body. This man was very common with no special internal additions to speak of.

Severing the head was also a simple matter and going through the vertebrae in the back of the neck didn't take much at all by going through connective tissue.

The torso was surprisingly heavy all by itself and I cut that in two across the diaphragm. Human intestines just look like one long roll of uncooked sausage as opposed to the gruesome millage of stringy nastiness they appear to be on film. I was surprised. Funny sounds and pressure releases took place on my table as the torso sank.

Once the body was in bags, I started my cleanup process. I took down the plastic walls from my bubble which surprisingly had almost no spatter on them. Then I started to roll the plastic on the table up and to my chagrin, noticed it had very little effect in keeping the blood off the tables steel surface. I soldiered on, cleaning up all of the plastic. I tore my green cloth backdrop down and placed it over the larger blood pools on the floor after I picked up the soaked coat and trashed it.

The green backdrops went into the trash next and then I began my stain removal process. I had two bottles of pure ammonia that I dabbed into paper towels to wipe away small stains. The spatter was everywhere. There were dozens of small spots on the floor and tiny streaks on the walls and big door. I wiped them all away. The great thing about ammonia is that even if the stain won't completely wipe away, it destroys the sample so that no DNA can be processed. It also eats fingerprints like acid. It's only downside is the fumes, which I didn't smell so much as feel like a cold winter breeze shooting its way through my sinuses.

I kept away from it and wore masks whenever possible. I wiped my table clean, scrubbed the areas on the floor that needed it, wiped my computer table down and noticed a few tiny spots had made it onto my laptop. I was not impressed but knew they would be easy to spot clean.

Next time, the whole room gets bubbled, not just the half for my kill room. I had used a plastic sheeting normally chosen to cover living room furniture when painting walls, but it obviously didn't suffice. This time I used a single layer of mid grade quality stuff. Next time I would double layer the high grade material for sure.

The One Who Got Away

When I got finished I looked down in horror at the sheer level of blood staining my clothes from head to toe. I couldn't walk back into the house like this. I mean I had extra clothes in my car I could change into, that wasn't the point. But surely there would be a smell and I couldn't get all the blood off my face, not all of it.

My phone rang. The familiar buzzing of it's vibrate setting going off. The caller ID showed it was Tess calling. What could I do? I answered.

"Hi baby, what's up?"
"Not much. Where are you?" "I'm just leaving the gym hun."
'The gym closes at nine."

I checked my watch hurriedly, it showed 9:57pm. My mind raced. I couldn't get caught in a lie. Not again.

"What are you talking about babe? It closes at ten." "The big gym by our place?"

And there was my window. I had switched gyms when we moved to our new house so it sorted itself out as I jumped back in to play the game. "No, my old gym babe."

"I thought you cancelled that membership a month ago."

"I procrastinated ..."as I do tend to do quite often. "and did it a few weeks ago but I still have a couple weeks this month that are paid for so I figured I'd take advantage since it takes an hour to cross town anyway."

My wife is not stupid. It takes a lot to convince her of an elaborate lie. When she caught me surfing internet dating sites, I spun this quick tale of how I was just research an article on online dating I got through a free lance website. Fortunately for me, I really was a member of the free lance site already and could prove that part.

The next part was much harder. She wanted proof upon proof. I had to manufacture an entire person which is a lot more hassle than it sounds. I created a fake employer, ran out to get a prepaid cell phone and then hired an actor to do a role play on the phone with me, on speaker so Tess could hear it. Then I had him leave a voicemail message as this person so that if she called the number it would sound legit.

I went through great lengths to bring my wife over to the comfortable belief I wasn't cheating on her, but me hiding anything was the problem. Even safely believing in my fidelity didn't matter next to he dishonesty of hiding the article from her in the first place. And so our trust issues flared up again. Now every conversation was an interrogation. Not just a simple question where she could take my answer at my word. There had to be back checking involved. So I waited for her response to my explanation and after a short breath ...

"Ok, well listen on your way home can you pick up a case of ready made baby formula at Shoppers?"

"Will do. Anything else?" In my mind I begged for her not to ask me to get her a late night latte. That's all I needed was to walk into a Starbucks in mismatching attire, dried blood across my face and hands. That sort of thing people notice, even if they feel too awkward to ask questions.

"No, but I'll probably be in bed by the time you get home. I'm so tired." She said with a yawn. Finally a break. A dark silent home to come to where I can go straight into the basement, throw my coat, hoody, pants, shoes, socks and shirt straight into the laundry and shower any remnants off of me.

"Fantastic. I'll see you tomorrow then." "Kay, bye."

I packed up my laptop bag and then opened the garage door, half expecting a team of police cruisers to be waiting outside, but the alley was empty and silent save for the Mazda parked in the driveway. I took the keys and got in. A fucking manual transmission. I had never learned how to drive them but necessity is the mother of invention after all. I probably stalled the damn thing a good ten times before enough trial and error got me to the point where I could manage to get the stupid thing inside the garage.

I laid a plastic sheet across the hatchback floor and put the body bags in the trunk. At least the car was clean and empty. After a quick search I found Jims cell phone, turned it off to avoid pings sent from the police to track it and made sure there was no GPS turned on either. I locked up the garage, went out to my car under cover of night and changed clothes, stuffing the blood soaked ones into my duffle bag. I changed shoes as well. Another glance at my watch gave me the realization the store would be closed by the time I got there and sure enough, by the time I reached the other side of town I was way too late to buy formula. It was the last of my worries.

I decided to wake up early and run out to the store to grab the formula before the baby woke up but I was so bagged from the events of the night before that I overslept and had to make up something to the warden about them being out of stock last night when I went which allowed me to make the trip Saturday morning.

I had a pretty normal Saturday. Watching the kid so Tess could get some personal stuff tended to, having a bit of a break from the constant supervision of a young infant, cute as she was.

Zoe had always been exceptionally adorable and it wasn't just us biased parents who thought so. Everyone at the hospital was of the same opinion and every time Tess ran errands, the ladies at the bank would swoon over Zoe like she was the second coming of Christ in a female package. She charmed everyone who met her. She softened the hardened selfish prick that was Tess' father, and won over several others who until meeting Zoe, had not been "kid people" at all. The final confirmation of that was when mother and daughter had gone to get her first professional pictures taken and even the people at the photo studio who dealt with children all day every day noted how exceptionally happy and easy going she was.

Zoe was born mellow. When other kids are throwing tantrums in public she stares at them with a questioning as to what the hell could be wrong with them. She loves going places and was very early to alertness. When other babies were dough eyed or utterly confused, she was looking around, tracking everything and looking at people directly with curiosity.

She's a wonderful baby, an angel that we were spoiled to have with such an easy disposition. I really hope she doesn't end up like me. I watched an episode of Dexter where the flashback showed his father showing Dexter CAT scans of a human brain. He identified the differences between a serial killers brain and a normal persons brain.

Up until I saw that I was convinced that what I was, was my own decision, my own path but now I truly wondered if I had little choice at all, and if genetics play a bigger role than I thought.

Logically then it should have occurred to me that those traits have a possibility of being passed to my offspring. I do have hope for Zoe though. My parents are certainly not like me so there's no guarantee on generational transition, and she is also half Tess and I've never seen such empathy, moral code or ethical sturdiness as I have in her.

Quite the odd couple Tess and I. On a couple of occasions we even discussed my apparent total lack of empathy and it troubled her greatly. She asked me a long series of probing and somewhat leading questions to see if I would give her the answer she desired but I never did.

"When you see news stories of people going through tremendous grief or strife, do you feel bad for them?"

"No."

"Do you ever think about what it would be like if that were your family in that situation?"

"It's never crossed my mind." was my answer and it continued like this until Tess was satisfied her husband couldn't feel much of anything at all I imagine. I did calm her fears though by at least reassuring her that I did care very much about her and Zoe and that neither of them would ever feel unloved.

I do love my daughter very much. She brings me great joy, and I love playing games with her. If anyone ever threatened her happy innocent existence in any way I would kill them, cut the body up and make it disappear. Most people say that about their children, only I actually mean it literally.

Sunday was all set up for more family merriment, much like the Saturday before it. I began to get itchy though and wanted to move on to the next part of my overall plan for Jim. I woke up at the crack of dawn, 5:00 am and left the house. Neither of the ladies would be up for another three hours and I had a person to erase.

I drove across town to the South side, not for the kill room this time, but for the home of my victim. I found his place without pause, parked in front of the building, careful to examine surroundings and make sure that there was no video surveillance. It was still early morning and comings and goings were common in the area.

I wore my hoody to cover my head and face, and my gloves to leave prints out of the situation entirely. My shoes had just come out of the dryer and were spotless. They would leave no imprints anywhere inside the apartment. I used his keys to enter the building, cautiously watching for video surveillance and strolled down the hallway until I found the door I needed.

I paused for a moment, better not to take chances. I knocked first, just in case for whatever reason, there was someone inside. There wasn't and slowly I entered the place closing and locking the door behind me. A simple one bedroom apartment. Somewhat clean save for a few dishes left out. It represented a single man perfectly. Motor cycle gear, a big screen TV, a computer desk, a nice barbecue and some online gaming machinery.

I found cash on the dresser which quickly found its way into my wallet. I searched drawers and shelves for anything else of interest, putting everything back as it was. Then I sat down at the computer desk. I wasn't sure what I would find. I was hoping some basic searches would yield passwords or something but Jim had done me one better. He left himself signed in to everything. Messenger, outlook express, his online dating profile and his facebook all had the passwords auto saved.

I couldn't have had an easier time. I changed the auto response on his email to say he had decided to run away with the woman he hooked up with on Friday to go on a two month vacation to the Caribbean. I changed the status on his facebook account to reflect the change and then I proceeded to delete his online dating profile. Judging by his email content it seemed he was on several sites at once so that trail would go cold real quickly.

My phone rang. It was Tess again asking where I was. I said I had gone to my parents to pick up a few tools for working on the downstairs bathroom and that I would be back in an hour. Conversation over. I had an after thought. What if the police ever did track this back to me and checked my cell phone records? They would see the towers my phone picked its signal up from and notice I was in the area. If the garage I rented wasn't already a few streets away that might be a problem.

I packed Jims laptop up and took it with me. I also took his multifunction printer and threw it into a dumpster because the email I sent him with directions to my kill room had been printed on it and it wouldn't do to have that be recoverable by the police. But I did find something in the printer that would help. A letter to his insurance company with a clear unmarked signature on white background.

It was one last gift from the dead. I could easily use that to forge a bill of sale for the car. If the authorities ever questioned me about it I could corroborate my own story. "Yeah officer it was the strangest thing. This guy approaches me on the street and tells me he met this phenomenal woman, a real sugar mamma who is going to take care of him and that he doesn't need his car anymore. So he asks me how much I have on me and when I tell him I've only got twenty three bucks, he says 'ok deal' and I end up with a free car."

Armed with my new toys and info I headed home. My next problem was what to do with the body. I mean it's not like I had an ocean to dump it in, or a boat for that matter. What did that leave? When you live in a land locked city what are your options for making two hundred and thirty pounds of dead human go away?

Incineration. I had looked into buying an actual batch incinerator. Something with the pressure and heat needed to get the job done. The problem with those are that they cost upwards of five thousand dollars to acquire and I wouldn't be in a position to make that purchase for another month or two. I had a jerry can of gasoline in my trunk and a steel drum though. Close enough.

Monday morning and I had some free time to myself, at least until about 4:30 in the afternoon when the wife expected me to be back home. To keep the illusion of my day job up, I would leave earlier on Mondays to pretend I had to be in a Monday morning meeting.

I went straight to my kill room. I lined my trunk with plastic sheeting and stuffed the body bags in. I laid the drum across the back seat and stuffed my garbage bags into it to save space and extra trips. I took everything to my parents house. They were gone during the day and had a nice fenced back yard for privacy.

My arms were very sore. Maybe the athletic event leading into the weekend had been quite jarring but I was experiencing shooting pain that was clearly the result of pinched nerves in my back. I didn't have the time or money to see a chiropractor but I would use the massage chair I gave my wife for Christmas one year several times later that night.

In the meantime though, everything was a chore. Lifting the barrel, lifting the bags out of the trunk; they were all accompanied by soreness and agitation. At some points my arms would recoil sharply in exhaustion from pushing them no further than what felt like an average hoisting.

I doused the first bag which contained the torso pieces in gasoline after dropping it into the barrel. I lit a match and tossed it in. The instant whoosh of flames consuming flammable liquid exploded from the top and the burn began. I had placed the barrel squarely in the center of the yard. It was broad daylight but everything was sealed in bags so no one could see anything, especially not the burning process.

I've heard that there is no smell like that of a burning fleshy person. If I had a sense of smell I may have taken note but I lack that particular member of the five sense group so you won't get any dramatic descriptions from me.

I imagine it smells like barbecue steak mixed with singed hair. When you cut up a person you realize we are really no different than animals. We're just sacks of meat at the end of the day. The internal muscles and tissues of the human body look a whole lot like steak actually. In fact, if properly trimmed and packaged, I believe most people would have a hard time telling them apart.

Maybe they taste different but I never felt the compulsion to cross that line. I could see the curiosity that Dahmer had and I understand the mentality behind why he did it, I just don't think that way and I'm not about to eat any meat that's been dead and sitting out for days, regardless of the source. It tends to change how one views a sirloin when it comes to the table though.

I checked on my burning waste and added more gas. Not straight out of the jerry can of course, I'm not up for any Darwin awards. I poured some into a coffee cup and dumped accordingly. I repeated that three times when I realized it wasn't doing anything. The pain in my arms became merely the start of my problems.

My biggest issue now was the complete lack of effectiveness this method of disposal had.

As if that weren't bad enough I heard sirens. Now in my kill rooms neighborhood sirens are customary and you know it's time to worry when you don't hear them on a nightly basis. But in this nice sweet little schoolyard area, sirens mean something significant. Someone spotted the smoke and called the fire department. I now had two very big reasons to put the fire out.

I doused the fire in water extinguishing it immediately. The smoke dissipated and almost as if the fire crew knew exactly what was happening, the sirens stopped. It could have been a massive coincidence but I heavily doubted it. All I knew was that having the fire crew pull up to the house and start poking around was not an option. Granted a charred and cut up torso looks somewhat similar to a couple pieces of big beef but any closer inspection would expose me and that wouldn't do.

When the smoke cleared I found that the bag had melted and some of the edges were charred but for the most part, the body was still in tact, some of the skin hadn't even been cooked. I knew there was no way the organs were affected. It would take a week to burn the waste unrecognizable at this pace and use more gas than I could afford. So I re-bagged everything, loaded it back into the car and took it back to the kill room.

Realizing that incineration was out completely I had to change strategies. I decided to cut the body into smaller pieces and dump it in the river that ran straight through middle of the city creating an impromptu border between the North and South sides of town. I didn't have time for that the same afternoon, it would have to wait a day or two.

After the days activities were complete I headed home a little earlier. I played with Zoe, watching her while Tess took a shower and relaxed. I fed the child dinner, gave her a bath and then it would be time for her to go to sleep. Zoe slept straight through the night only a week after she was born. The kid loves sleeping and by seven months on the planet she was out for twelve straight hours every night starting at 7:30pm. Like I said, lucky.

As Tess settled in on the living room couch to watch her evening programs I jumped on the computer. Laci was online and I began chatting with her. At first it was cordial, loosely discussing plans to get together again. I was looking forward to having her again and I know she felt the same way. We were both getting impatient and it was showing in our conversations.

Neither one of us had experienced sex nearly as good as each others in the eight years we had been apart. Her relationships were with pathetic losers who preferred playing online games over actual human affection and when they did get in the mood, they lasted for only a couple minutes at a time. I never understood how a guy can cum so easily with so little self control lasting less than ten minutes in a session. I always loved taking my time and Laci felt the same way.

My first marriage was heated all the way through but this meant the fighting was just as intense as the love making and it became too much to handle. Besides I got married for all the wrong reasons the first time, getting into a relationship just because I thought I was ready. I was very young, only twenty one at the time and too stupid to realize the truth. My wife was less attractive than me, and a little overweight but cute.

At any rate it didn't last. The second best sexual experience I ever had was with a Laotian girl I was essentially using for my rebound, but of course she didn't see it that way. She was under the impression we were a long term thing and we might have been if I wasn't so screwed up. She could hold her own in the marathons and would actually say (almost out of breath) after we were done "How can anyone go for three hours straight?"

So when Laci popped up on the instant messenger inviting me to her place for a late night rendezvous I did everything in my power to make it happen. I knew I would need to wait until Tess was in bed so I could safely sneak out. I could easily spend the night at Laci's house since I could pass off not being there in the morning as getting an early start.

But even though Tess was tired and wanting to go to bed early, it just didn't happen. She stayed up, delaying my departure and I knew there was a solid hour and a half drive time to get to Laci's. As Tess was going to bed I took my computer bag into the living room telling her I was going to stay up and write for awhile. She accepted that with no reserve and went to bed.

In two minutes I was out the door. I jumped into the car and headed out to Lacis as fast as I could. Too fast in fact. I was pulled over for speeding on the freeway. I did another round of top notch acting pretending to give a shit about breaking the posting limit and begged for him to go easy on me. He gave me a ticket anyway but at least it was less than half the price it could have been and I also appreciated how quick he was about it. I was back on the road in five minutes flat.

I remember thinking how hilarious and dramatically ironic it was that the cop had pulled over a cold blooded murderer who had a dismembered body in his rented garage not too far away and had no clue what was going on. He just did his duty and took off. Now every time I pass a police car on the road I chuckle to myself.

I got to Lacis without further incident. She let me inside dressed in her pajamas and no sooner had I dropped my bag on the floor than we were making out intensely. We moved to her bedroom and shut the door to keep her dogs out. We kissed passionately in juicy anticipation of what was coming next. She lay on her bed and opened the pajamas to reveal a sexy set of white lingerie style underwear. The bottoms were a thong which always gets me insanely turned on.

----- SKConfessions[1].docx -----OVERLAP----- - WRL0334.tmp ----

Laci looked better than I had ever remembered her. A decade ago at the tender age of twenty four she was gorgeous but still not as fine as she looked this very night in question. She had been hitting the gym, gone tanning to prepare for her vacation and had taken up the hobby of belly dancing. I have never been a fan of scrawny girls. In my opinion if you can see ribs poking through the skin the woman needs a hefty helping of cheeseburgers very badly. Laci was beautiful, sensual with curves in all the right places. Now she was the ideal textbook form of what a woman should look like with the added skill of how to rotate her hips in ways most women only dream they could.

Her large deep green eyes stared seductively into mine and I couldn't resist her even if I tried, not that I would want to try. Being with her took on the pace of quickly catching up to how we used to be.

Laci and I explored each other for a good two hours that night trying several positions, all of them making both of us crazy. I was free to suck on various parts of her body and go down on her for as long as she could take it before needing me inside her again. The way she felt, the way she tasted, all so familiar and so amazing to have again. She came to orgasm four times before I let myself get to the same place and when we were done there was no describing the contentment we experienced.

I laid there next to her gently stroking her hair and back. I examined the tattoo on her left shoulder blade, the one I had designed for her in college. It was a celtic knot style cross with vines intertwined within it; a beautiful piece, inked by a real master. Her second; placed on the back of her neck acquired at the same location, was done by someone clearly less experienced since its lines were not perfect and the shading slightly out of balance. It still looked good from a few feet away but this close up it didn't compete with the first.

She remembered mine too. The one on my left shoulder I had gotten while dating her all those years ago. It had since been retouched and I was physically much bigger from filling out as an adult and frequent trips to the gym. Maybe it was me being of a larger stature than my thin teenage self of the past, but she seemed smaller this time. My other two tattoos were more recent and new additions to her.

Some of our past together was as clear as day to Laci. Other elements were lost to her. She had gone on a vacation to a third world tropical country and brought back with her a virus that attacked her brain. She had been ill for two years as a result and it could have ended much worse with some sort of organic brain dementia or even death coming for her. She escaped with her health and her faculties, as well as this smoking hot new body.

I fell asleep next to her and when I awoke in the morning, she had to be at work in the city, whereas I had nowhere to be. So I slept in, she left me a spare key and when I was ready I got ready to leave. Her dogs woke up to greet me. They are small annoying little things that she treats as if they were human children, which I never understood but could easily respect since for years they were the only constant source of unconditional love and acceptance in her world.

In my opinion, a dog is something roughly the size of a German shepherd that you can actually wrestle with and take on walks without fear that a bird of prey will snatch it up like a squirrel and run it off to feed it to its young, but that's just me. These two uppity things would bark at any average Joe walking down the street and I couldn't wait to get out of there.

Laci had left the TV on so I turned it off, thinking that it would obviously be a tremendous waste of energy since I highly doubted a dog could get anything out of watching The View. I packed up my things, and left her spare key under a statue on her front porch before I took off for the day. I had work to do.

break.

It was time to assess the situation again. I had a hatchback with body parts in the trunk locked inside a garage I still had to sweep clean. I had waste to dispose of and tracks to erase. I had no idea who this guy had talked to in the interim periods between his first arrival at my lair and his last, so for all I knew some friend of his out there could even have the exact address or at the very least detailed descriptions of how to get there.

If I ever figured out a safe, quick way of rendering my victims unconscious at another location without witnesses or forensic evidence left behind, I would do that. But for now this system was fine as long as I stuck to strict adherence of the plan. I headed straight for my kill room to deal with my mess.

First things first, I grabbed breakfast from a Dennys that was just up the street from my sanctuary. My moons-over-my-hammy was especially delicious and I just had to stop by a 7-11 to pick up a chocolate milk and a large French vanilla latte. This meal would keep me satisfied for at least a couple hours. I made sure to pick up some snacks for the day as well.

When I arrived on the street of my kill room I approached cautiously, as always just in case. As each time prior there was no fanfare of police and ambulance gathered around the front or the back. No one had accidentally found anything and called it in. No weird smells were emitting from the place and very well shouldn't be considering everything was sealed and still fresh.

I got inside and prepped for what my day would be like. The nights rest had numbed the great majority of my nerve pain and I felt fine to continue. I began by taking the bags out of the Mazda and placing them on the floor next to my butcher table. I double sheeted the table this time, placed my processing kit, my cleaver and the galvanized pipe at one end, my ammonia cleaning supplies and paper towels on the other. I placed plastic sheeting around the table on the floor as well and moved the steel drum over within leaning distance with a brand new empty hefty bag in it to catch the waste.

The next step was to prep myself. I wouldn't allow any blood and guts to get on me today. I used some of my plastic sheeting and duct tape to fashion a makeshift apron for myself. I picked up new much higher grade plastic abrasive cleaner resistant gloves and then duct taped two grocery bags around my shoes to keep them clean also. I wore a basic white painters mask to keep fumes away from me and take some of the edge off the ammonia smell.

I picked up the first bag and set it on the table. I put my cutting board on the table, to prevent my knives from accidentally puncturing or tearing holes in my plastic sheeting which I suspected may have played a role in drenching my table surface last time. I had previously closed the bags by twisting the ends and wrapping the tightest part with duct tape so this time I just cut them open with the short knife.

I took out one of the arms. It was stiff and cold, rigor mortis having set in by now. It was also quite brisk outside today since it was fall heading into winter. I was grateful for the temperature though since my outfit was warm and I would be doing quite a bit of physical activity today.

I chose the butcher knife to start out with and simply shaved the meat from the bone in a downward motion. I didn't bother getting every single shred, since I knew that once dumped in the river, it would rot off in a timely fashion anyway. When it was cleared, each slab looked like a cutlet sitting on the table.

I put each chunk on the cutting board and used the fillet knife to slice them into even smaller pieces. When I was satisfied with my medallion sized portions, I tossed them into the garbage bag. Very little mess was made at first.

I repeated the process with the legs, thighs and upper arms. Routinely shaving the meat off them, placing the bones in a pile and filleting the meat into small pieces before tossing them into the bag. When the bag got somewhat heavy to lift easily, I closed it off in the same fashion as the originals and got a new one.

Once in a while I would take a break, check my email, answer a few phone calls, check the status of my ebay page and have a bag of chips. I got a message from Laci on Facebook commenting on how hot the night was and how she was looking forward to the next time. I fantasized about the night before and how Laci had been a total porn star in the sack. I was incredibly lucky. When I realized two hours had passed I decided to get the rest of the waste dealt with as soon as possible so I could take as much of the afternoon off as possible.

Every couple of body parts, I would need to clean and sharpen my knives since they were doing a lot of work going through so much material. I decided to do the head next. I sliced the face off in several different pieces, cut the ears and lips up so that again, they couldn't be visually identified. This way if someone did see it floating in a river, they would think nothing of it anyway.

Once the flesh was removed, I used the pipe to knock out the teeth, eliminating dental records as a form of ID. I broke the jaw after that and used the scissors to cut the ligaments, ripping the jaw clean from the head in it's multiple pieces held together only by the tissue at this point. I used the knife to destroy the eyes as well and then rammed the pipe into the side of the skull to bust it open. At this point it was fueled only by a curiosity to see the human brain live and in person since I had never seen it before.

I realized I was spending too much time on the head and tossed it into a new hefty bag to move on. Next came the two heavy torso pieces. My arm pain flared up hoisting them to the table and then subsided by simply mentally pushing it out of the way. I began with the lower portion. I removed the intestines first, carved out the reproductive organs and anything else taking up space. Then I shaved the meat off the hip bones for as much would come off.

Removing the skin and flesh in the back was easy. These were the chunks I tried to burn the first time around so the skin was charred in some places making it more stiff in some places and easy to cut. I hacked off the ass cheeks and marveled at how fatty they were for such a slim person. I immediately thought of the movie Alive and how well the rugby team must have feasted on this part of the human body while trapped in the Andes. But the freezer burn from the bodies being in the snow and frozen solid might have ruined the experience. Well that and the trauma of realizing you're eating a dead person but that never entered my thinking at all. Meat is meat after all. It all tastes like beef or chicken.

Once that was processed, I moved on to my final piece, the upper torso. I started with shaving the outside, taking all of the skin, muscle and fat in single passes, like I was carving a turkey. In fact once everything else had been removed, I was surprised at how closely the chest cavity resembles the overall shape of a turkey.

This was the messy portion. All of the blood that hadn't come out was inside this piece, trapped in the lungs, still close to the heart. It dumped out onto the table, not quite enough to overflow to the floor or anything but messy nonetheless. I used a knife to cut all the tissue around the inside edge of the rib cage in order to free any remaining organs. The lungs, the heart and the liver all came out. I cut those up too before trashing them.

It reminded me of emptying a pumpkin for Halloween. Somehow every single event in life would have a whole new level of perspective to it. Carving a pumpkin and spilling its guts would now carry a double meaning. So would slicing up a steak, carving a Thanksgiving turkey or laying plastic down to prepare for painting the family room.

This experience changed my sense of place in the world forever. I felt stronger, somehow above other people. I felt like the proud owner of a very dark secret that no one would ever be in on. Things that I said to people would carry double entendres like they hadn't before. "Oh honey work was murder today." would be more literal than Tess would ever know.

When the body was dealt with I used paper towels to soak up much of the blood spill on the table so it wouldn't flow onto unprotected floor in the clean up process. My makeshift outfit went into a separate trash bag, one designated for secondary waste, not body parts. All table plastic and surrounding plastic got rolled up and tossed accordingly. At first it appeared my double sheeting on the table did it's job but upon final reveal, it turned out I needed to scrub with the stain remover again. High grade stuff next time, for sure.

I felt good about this. My plan now involved simply waiting for dark to come so I could visit a bridge. I opened the garage door, satisfied that nothing conspicuous was showing to the outside and unlocked my car, which I had parked closer to the back door this time for easy transfer. I layed new plastic in my car trunk and placed the new bags in one at a time. I closed up shop and headed for home.

It's an interesting feeling, driving around town with what used to be a human body bagged up in your trunk. No one has any idea they are stopped at a light right next to a serial killer with what could very well be one of their friends now sacks of meat parts in a hidden compartment. It made me wonder, in all my ten years of driving around, had I ever unknowingly passed a vehicle or sat parked at a red light next to someone just like I would be one day? It blew my mind.

I stuck to the posted speed limits, signaled when I changed lanes and didn't push any yellow lights whatsoever. I'm convinced that car insurance companies would get exceedingly rich from not paying claims and hospital traffic would slow to a crawl on major holidays if everyone drove as if they had a dead man in their trunk and a mortal fear of going to jail for twenty to life in the event they ever got pulled over and a police man decided to check their cars contents.

I got home without incident and went through my evening routine with ease. I hopped on the instant messenger to find Laci online. Only this conversation was not a happy one at all, it had taken a terrible turn for the worse. She was horribly depressed from reflecting on her past relationship situations and behaving erratically. She said she couldn't continue to see me because she was messed up and didn't want to put that on me, even though I expressly said to her that her and I could take things at whatever pace she felt comfortable with.

But it was more than that. Laci had discovered her ex husband met the clinical definition of a sociopath. The epiphany didn't come from consulting a psychiatrist, it came from finding a detailed article on the internet that outlined what male sociopaths do to the women they shack up with. In it she found all of his most redeeming qualities. Chronic pathological lying, using and abusing his partner, scamming everyone around him, treating other people with a total lack of respect or regard for their well being. What really pushed her over the edge was reading all the traits of women who usually fall for people like this and brought the problem onto herself. She was certain there were several things terribly wrong with her and tonight that had spiraled into contemplating suicide.

I was completely taken by surprise and had no idea what to do. This wasn't her usual bummed out attitude when reflecting on the years wasted with the idiots who couldn't appreciate her: both her ex husband and the boyfriend she had shortly after whom she had recently dumped for neglecting her and mistreating her much the same way. This was different. She was repeating back to me something I had said about how those who threaten suicide usually don't mean it unless they have a specific plan laid out.

That's when I panicked. She talked about pills, wondering what four would do and I remember thinking it depended entirely on what the pill was, the difference between sickness and death. I couldn't take chances. I begged her not to do it and used every phrase to desuade her, until the words "too late" popped onto my screen.

I did the only thing I could think of that was left. I picked up my phone and dialled 911.

"911 emergency."

"Hi, I've just been chatting online to a friend who has threatened suicide." "Ok what's your name sir?"
"Darren Ascot." It was obviously not my real name but that was irrelevant.
"And your friends name?" "Laci Barret."
"And where are you sir?"

"I'm in Bloomington heights." "And where is she?"
"She lives in Whetstone."

"How long have you known her?" "Ten years."
"Did she say why she's doing this or how?"

"She didn't specify why." which was true. She didn't say and my guesses were still only assumptions. "She talked about pills."

"Do you have her address?" I answered with the exact numbered address of where she lived. "Ok we're sending people out right now."

"Thank you." Just in case Laci was still awake I got back on the instant messenger and typed in 'I just called 911.' She responded shocked and appalled. She said I was being ridiculous and I asked her what else she could possibly expect me to do under the circumstances. The next message was hilarious.

'You are adding to my stress level' to which I could only reply ..

'YOUR stress level?' She was emotional and crashing and it was completely understandable. Her ex husband fit the sociopath profile draining her of all her self esteem, leaving her wondering if she was an alien or something. To follow it up her most recent boyfriend was in his early thirties still living at home with his mother and had abused and neglected her in the same way, blowing her off throughout their entire relationship and regularly cheating on her.

But that wasn't enough for this clown. When she finally mustered the courage to dump him once and for all, he had the sickening gall to prey on her compassionate nature by sending her countless messages begging to get her back. He didn't do it because he genuinely cared about her needs or health, only to control and manipulate her using her bleeding heart to her own detriment.

Laci showed me his messages and they instantly reminded me of a four year old throwing a temper tantrum to get what he wants from parents who haven't established clear rules and consequences. Everything was 'I need, I want, you need to give me' rather than any of it being about her. With my consolation and step by step coaching and translation of his true meaning and intentions, I helped her decode his bullshit.

While she was with him her sleep patterns were horribly disrupted. She woke up at all times during the night in cold sweats, had to wear mouth guards to stop her teeth from being worn away by grinding and she was on anti depressants which weren't even appropriate for her bodies chemistry. This guy did a real number on her and he was ever so close to being next on my short list.

Getting his personal information from her had been exceedingly easy. I would email her questions like 'what's his street address?', 'What's his full name?' and 'What's his email address?' I expected a tiny amount of screening from her like asking me why I wanted to know but all I got was direct answers, almost like she was encouraging me. I doubt the information would have been so readily available if she knew the intimate details of my new hobby.

I don't copy cat the style of Dexter Morgan. I don't have steady access to high power tranquilizers or the free time to stalk someone to get to know their routine well enough. I also don't keep souvenirs or trophies so I don't own a rosewood box with blood slides or anything quaint like that. My butchering tools are also more hands on rather than going powered since high speed spinning devices tend to make more spatter mess and I'd like to avoid a total blood bath if I can.

Laci sent me an email the next morning apologizing for the hurtful things she said to me when I had called the response units. She regaled me with her tales of how the night went, the psych pro they sent and the adventures of being poked prodded, examined and so forth. I was just glad to hear she still had a pulse. I told her she could repay me for saving her life by never doing that ever again.

Laci has people in her life besides me who love her and depend on her. Even those two runt mutts would lose their spoiled lifestyle with her gone. I just couldn't stand the thought that a pig like Evan would be the reason she took her own life. He was so much lower than scum on the food chain that it would be nothing short of tragic to pay him any kind of compliment by making him think he was that important or had that much impact on anyone's life. And he was messed up enough to take it as a compliment too.

The night had taken a lot out of me so far and I just wasn't up to dumping a body out in the middle of nowhere. I was blasted so I decided to hit the sack and get up early to do it in the morning. It was halfway through fall anyway and it would stay dark until 8:00am. If I got up at five, I'd have more than enough time to get the job done.

My alarm clock woke me up gently to the soft sounds of the easy rock station. That beeping noise all alarm clocks have drives aggravation and annoyance into my bone marrow when I hear it. Even when they use it in commercials I want to throw a brick at my television and that's just no way to start the day. Maybe Rod Stewart and a couple of DJ's who are mistaken about how funny they are isn't much better but it's a lot easier on the brain pan.

I geared up, got everything I needed to get going including a simple steak knife to cut the bags open quickly and silently moved through the house and out the door. It's moments like that that made me glad I had done little home improvement tasks like spraying WD40 in the hinges to eliminate the creaking. I got into my car and took off. There were two bridges over the same river I knew how to get to off the top of my head that would make suitable locations for the dump.

I got to the freeway bridge at the stroke of five thirty. It was still pitch black with no sun in sight. Right away I knew I couldn't do this from the bridge itself. There wasn't enough shoulder to stop without turning on my hazard lights and that would have attracted a cop car like a moth to a flame. There just wasn't anywhere to hide.

Coming off the bridge though there was a path marked by a sign that showed me a potential boat dock. Although it was a lie with no boat dock visible, it could get me to the water. Upon closer inspection of the area though I realized it just wasn't suitable. The only way to get to the waters edge was by traversing a very steep slope covered in loose rocks and I would have bet money that lugging heavy hefty bags down it would have me slipping to serious injury without fail.

I also wasn't comfortable with the layout under the bridge. It was too dark to tell but there boxes everywhere that I couldn't identify and if I wasn't sure it wasn't a surveillance *camera, I didn't want to take the chance. I left the same way I came in and moved on to my next choice.*

This one

----WRL0334.tmp -----OVERLAP----- -WRL1459.tmp ----

was more rural, further out of town between two farming communities and would have been ideal except that by the time I got there my timing was no longer optimal. The early birds had come out to play and the commuters were getting an early start to beat the morning rush hour traffic. I was poached, having chosen sleep over peek timing and had to consider waiting yet again to get rid of this thing. I decided to head back to my parents place and recoup.

On the forty five minute drive I tried to search for a solution. I asked myself If burning wouldn't work and bridge drop was out, what other way could I dump these parts in a safe unseen way? Once again necessity is the mother of invention and my need to get rid of this evidence brought the solution to me like a child showing a parent their latest pencil crayon drawing.

The sewer. Of course, how obvious. No one ever goes down there. The body would rot away completely before anyone ever discovered the bones and by then it would be way too late to identify the person.

----- -WRL1459.tmp -----OVERLAP----- Carved Text-----

Once again everything got lighter. I grabbed breakfast at a coffee donut place and ate it in the car on the way to my destination. A banana nut muffin, a double chocolate donut and a cafe mocha. I love caffeinated beverages but I can't stand the taste of black coffee so as long as it can be dressed up not to taste like coffee, I'm all about it.

I chose the Eastern suburb of the city to dump my waste. It would be practically a ghost town with most of its residents either having commuted to work in the city or otherwise occupied and away from their homes. The housing in this part of my world was also older, done back in the sixties and seventies when neighborhoods were not so congested so there were back alleys to be had. Newer neighborhoods have the homes grouped so close together with attached garages facing the street that alleys don't exist in the new city plans anymore.

Within a few moments I found exactly what I was looking for; a manhole cover placed off to the side behind a power pole. I parked in an empty driveway and popped the trunk. Although it was broad daylight I wasn't worried. No one appeared to be around and I was checking throughout the entire process. Lifting the cover was a piece of cake and my arms gave me no complaint, the pain gone finally. I removed the hefty bags one at a time from the trunk and walked them over the three paces it took to reach the sewer.

With each bag I sliced the tops off and turned them upside down letting the pieces fall into the sewer hearing the splashing sounds as they touched down. I crumpled the bags up, put them back in the trunk and then closed it. I got back in the car, fired her up and took off. My total time there could not have been longer than three minutes max.

I drove back to the kill room to finish destroying evidence. Once there, I packed my trunk remnants into a garbage bag and put everything else in there that needed to burn. Documents from Jims car, receipts, even my empty chip bags. I had five full hefty bags full of garbage that actually would burn, this I knew for a fact. Plastic sheeting, cloth backdrops and paper towels. It may not have been good for the environment but one less person creating pollution for whatever forty some odd more years he would have walked the Earth more than evens that out.

It was funny. This time I burned garbage for a solid three hours making sure nothing was left and did not hear a single siren in a neighborhood where sirens are as common as the sound of a bus stopping and going again. I suppose if my shit hole of an unheated rented detached garage goes up in smoke, no one gives a rats ass, and I was sure there had to be the areas fair share of unemployed people or passersby to call it in if they really wanted to.

To be fair though, plastic burns a lot more colorless than attempted flesh and the smoke was barely visible. The only irritant I had to contend with were the garbage trucks making their rounds up and down the alleys. Every time they would come past I'd have to lid my drum, snuff out my fire, drag it back into the garage and close the door to avoid unwanted attention and then drag it back out and start the process over again.

Gilles Tetreault

I used the gas from my jerry can again, soaked all the garbage

About the Author

Gilles Tetreault is a first time author of the book *The One Who Got Away*, which is based on his personal journey from the assault of convicted murderer, Mark Twitchell. After his incredible ordeal, he has made appearances on Dateline NBC, 48 Hours Mystery, The Fifth Estate, True Crime Canada, I Survived, Dates from Hell and The Security Brief with Paul Viollis. Gilles is originally from Gravelbourg, Saskatchewan and currently lives in Edmonton, Alberta with his son Benjamin.

www.tetreault.org

www.facebook.com/GillesTetreaultAuthor

CPSIA information can be obtained
at www.ICGtesting.com
Printed in the USA
LVHW050922170623
750067LV00009B/631

9 781539 347736